# METRICS

| OUNCES | POUNDS | GRAMS | KILOGRAMS | |
|---|---|---|---|---|
| 1 OZ | | 30 G | | |
| 2 OZ | | 60 G | | |
| 3 OZ | | 85 G | | |
| 4 OZ | | 115 G | | AN EGG |
| 5 OZ | | 140 G | | THAT IS |
| 6 OZ | | 180 G | | REALLY STALE |
| 8 OZ | | 225 G | | WILL FLOAT |
| 9 OZ | | 250 G | 1/2 KG | OR |
| 10 OZ | | 285 G | | TIP UPWARD |
| 12 OZ | | 340 G | | IN |
| 14 OZ | | 400 G | | A BOWL |
| 16 OZ | 1 LB | 450 G | | OF WATER. |
| 18 OZ | 1 1/8 LB | 500 G | | |
| 20 OZ | 1 1/4 LB | 560 G | | WHEN |
| 24 OZ | 1 1/2 LB | 675 G | | CRACKED OPEN, |
| 28 OZ | 1 3/4 LB | 800 G | | IF |
| 32 OZ | 2 LB | 900 G | | THE WHITE |
| | 2 1/4 LB | 1000 G | 1 KG | AND YOLK |
| | 2 1/2 LB | 1125 G | 1 1/4 KG | CLING TOGETHER, |
| | 3 LB | 1350 G | 1 1/3 KG | THE EGG |
| | 3 1/2 LB | 1500 G | 1 1/2 KG | IS |
| | 4 LB | 1800 G | 1 3/4 KG | VERY FRESH. |
| | 4 1/2 LB | | 2 KG | |
| | 5 LB | | 2 1/4 KG | THE OLDER |
| | 5 1/2 LB | | 2 1/2 KG | IT GETS, |
| | 6 LB | | 2 3/4 KG | THE FLATTER |
| | 7 LB | | 3 1/4 KG | THE YOLK |
| | 8 LB | | 3 1/2 KG | BECOMES |
| | 9 LB | | 4 KG | AND |
| | 10 LB | | 4 1/2 KG | THE RUNNIER |
| | 12 LB | | 5 1/2 KG | THE WHITE, |
| | 14 LB | | 6 1/4 KG | |
| | 15 LB | | 6 3/4 KG | |
| | 16 LB | | 7 1/4 KG | |
| | 18 LB | | 8 KG | |
| | 20 LB | | 9 KG | |
| | 25 LB | | 11 1/4 KG | |
| | 50 LB | | 22 1/2 KG | |

TO PREVENT WHITE SAUCE FROM LUMPING, IT'S SAFER TO HAVE THE MILK HOT WHEN YOU ADD IT TO THE ROUX (THE FLOUR AND BUTTER MIXTURE). ALWAYS COOK YOUR ROUX A FEW MINUTES BEFORE ADDING LIQUID.

TO CORRECT A CURDLED OR BROKEN HOLLANDAISE OR MAYONNAISE SAUCE, WHISK IN A TEASPOON OR TWO OF BOILING WATER, A DROP AT A TIME. IF THAT DOESN'T WORK, PUT AN EGG YOLK IN A BOWL AND ADD THE "BROKEN" SAUCE SLOWLY, BEATING WITH A WHISK, AND IN TIME YOU'LL HAVE A SMOOTH SAUCE.

# Chef Joe's
# Most requested Recipes

2003 © Ramberg, Evans & Andersen publishing
First Edition

Chef:                  Joe Evans, Florida USA

Layout and photos:     Peter Andersen, Denmark
                       Trond Ramberg, Norway/USA

Editor:                Ryan Evans, Florida USA

Project coordinator:   Patricia Evans, Florida USA

Printing:              Wennbergs Trykkeri, Norway

Photos in this book were taken
on the keys of Florida's Gulf Coast.

ISBN: 0-9749294-0-9

1

# FORWARD

FOOD! FAMILY! FRIENDS! THEY ARE THE BULL'S EYES ON MY DART BOARD OF LIFE. I AM A VERY FORTUNATE MAN, HAVING BEEN BLESSED WITH A WONDERFUL FAMILY, FANTASTIC FRIENDS AND A PROFESSION THAT I TRULY LOVE — BEING A CHEF. THESE PAST THIRTY-FIVE YEARS HAVE BEEN AN AMAZING JOURNEY FOR ME. I HAVE WASHED DISHES IN ROADSIDE GREASY SPOONS, BUSSED TABLES IN SOUTH PHILLY SALOONS, FRIED FISH AT TOURIST TRAPS ALONG THE JERSEY SHORE, BROILED STEAKS AND CHOPS IN DINNER THEATRES, FED THE UPPER CRUST OF PHILADELPHIA'S BLUE BLOODS IN VARIOUS SOCIETY HILL BISTROS AND CAFES, CRACKED THE WHIP AS KITCHEN "RINGMASTER" FOR A MAJOR HOSPITAL, PREPARED BANQUETS AT ELEGANT SOUTHERN COUNTRY CLUBS AND CATERED ROMANTIC DINNERS FOR TWO AND GRAND OPENINGS FOR TWO THOUSAND. I'VE TRAVELED ACROSS THE COUNTRY AS A TROUBLE-SHOOTING CHEF FOR A LARGE HOTEL CHAIN, PUMPED OUT CAKES, PIES AND PASTRIES FOR AWARD WINNING RESTAURANTS, OWNED AND OPERATED CHEESE STEAK JOINTS, SEAFOOD HOUSES, BREAKFAST PLACES AND LUNCHEONETTES. I'VE PEDDLED SAUSAGES AND HOT DOGS ON THE PHILADELPHIA WATERFRONT TO LONGSHOREMEN AND TRUCK DRIVERS, DEMONSTRATED RECIPES AND FOOD EQUIPMENT IN FRONT OF LIVE AUDIENCES, AND PREPARED DINNER FOR FAMILIES IN FLORIDA MANSIONS. IT'S BEEN QUITE AN ADVENTURE. ALONG THE WAY, I'VE MET MANY INTERESTING PEOPLE AND MADE HUNDREDS OF FRIENDS AND ACQUIRED SO MANY ORIGINAL RECIPES THAT I COULD FILL THOUSANDS OF BOOKS.

THE INSPIRATION FOR MY CALLING CAME FROM THE NEIGHBORHOOD WHERE I GREW UP — SOUTH PHILADELPHIA. THE ROAD FROM THERE TO AN ISLAND OFF THE WEST COAST OF FLORIDA HAS BEEN WONDROUS, FILLED WITH GREAT STORIES, AMAZING PEOPLE AND ALWAYS FOOD, FOOD AND MORE FOOD.

A LOT OF THE RECIPES THAT I HAVE IN THIS BOOK ARE INFLUENCED BY MY EARLY DAYS AS A CHEF. I'VE ADDED SOME OF MY IDEAS AND THOSE OF MANY OTHERS. I DON'T EVER RECALL HAVING A PIECE OF GRILLED SALMON IN MY YOUNG LIFE BUT I WATCHED MY FATHER SQUEEZE FRESH LEMON ON A SIDE OF BLUEFISH ON THE BACKYARD BARBEQUE. I LOOKED AND I LISTENED AND I LEARNED. I PICKED AT THE KNOWLEDGE OF PREP COOKS AND CHEFS, ABSORBED COOKBOOKS LIKE THEY WERE BEST SELLING NOVELS, WORKED DAY AND NIGHT AT TIMES FOR NOTHING AND AT OTHER TIMES FOR MORE MONEY THAN I NEEDED — IT'S BEEN SWEET!

THE SELECTED DISHES IN THIS BOOK ARE FUN AND EASY TO PREPARE. THEY HAVE BEEN TESTED OVER MANY YEARS AND THEY ALL WORK WELL. I AM A PERSONAL CHEF FOR THE FAMILIES PICTURED IN THIS COOKBOOK AND THESE ARE SOME OF MY PREFERRED RECIPES AND THEIR FAVORITE FOODS. SIT BACK AND RELAX, ENJOY CHEF JOE'S MOST REQUESTED RECIPES AND THEN "GET COOKIN!"

CHEF JOE EVANS

## ACKNOWLEDGEMENTS

My most sincere appreciation to all who were involved in the completion of this project. Their insights, knowledge, thoughtfulness, caring and unselfishness made a dream come true. This book came from many different people. No one approached me with an idea or a format, but many of the people that I have known and cooked for over the years, especially the families featured in this book, would constantly say, "Joe, you need to write a book." Well, thanks to all of them for having faith in me. Here it is, my first cookbook: Chef Joe's Most Requested Recipes, a compilation of varied dishes that I absolutely love to prepare for friends and family.

I must say special thanks to Trond Ramberg who said to me, "Joe you have a book to write and I will help you do it." He and his wife, Julie, were our masters of design. What can I say about the photographic genius of Peter Andersen? Every picture tells a story and, in this book, the pictures look good enough to eat. Peter and his girlfriend, Le Thuy Thi Nguyen, worked so hard to make every featured dish look especially appetizing. I am so proud that my son Ryan, who is a great writer himself, did such a wonderful job with the editing. I couldn't have done this without my wife, Pat, who frequently works with me as an invaluable assistant. Zach Evans, my eleven-year-old son, was a trooper during this whole production, never complaining that schedules were upset, dinners delayed or that our family life took a crazy turn for a while. Mrs. Sylvia Thompson was a constant force behind the scenes. Marie Cecile, your calls spurred me on. Greg Erickson's legal counsel was truly appreciated. Pam Arlington, you always amaze me with your hard work and wonderful humor. Genuine thanks to Paul Brugger of the Star Fish Company Seafood Market & Restaurant and Karen Bell of A.P. Bell Fish Co., Inc. for the location shots and the freshly caught seafood provided.

The Bealls Corporation has been an important resource and partner in this book production. Special thanks to Karen Filips, Amy Lengyel, Gwen Bennett, Mary Beth Allen, Kathy Wilson & all store managers who have invited me to their openings. Fran Smith, how can I thank you for being such a good friend and providing props and production locations? Wolfgang and Kathy Webber let us use their beautiful condominium on Holmes Beach for one of our production sets. Dr. and Mrs. Albert, thank you for requesting these recipes. The guacamole and caesar recipes are dedicated to the Jacobs family. I have prepared these dishes for them many times over the years. Roger, Debbie, Shayna and Matt Danziger, we treasure your friendship and your help throughout the years. Last but not least – heartfelt thanks to all the families pictured in this book. They have invited me into their homes and kitchens and I value their friendships immensely.

# CONTENTS

## FAVORITES

## SWEETS

# Seafood Ceviche

(SERVES 4)

| | |
|---|---|
| 12 | LARGE SHRIMP, SHELLED, DEVEINED, WASHED THOROUGHLY |
| 12 | LARGE SEA SCALLOPS |
| 1/2 | LB. LUMP CRAB MEAT (PICKED CLEAN) |
| 1 | TSP. GARLIC, MINCED |
| 1 | SHALLOT, MINCED |
| 1 | JALAPEÑO PEPPER, SEEDED AND MINCED |
| 2 | TBSP. FRESH CILANTRO, CHOPPED |
| 1 | TSP. HOT SAUCE |
| 1 | TSP. KOSHER SALT |

JUICE OF 2 LEMONS
JUICE OF 2 LIMES
PINCH OF CAYENNE PEPPER
PINCH OF WHITE PEPPER

## PREPARATION

❏ PLACE SHRIMP AND SCALLOPS IN A GLASS BOWL AND SPRINKLE WITH KOSHER SALT AND WHITE PEPPER.

❏ ADD LEMON AND LIME JUICE, SHALLOTS, JALAPEÑOS, CAYENNE AND CILANTRO.

❏ MIX WELL, COVER AND REFRIGERATE FOR 24 HOURS.

❏ FOLD IN LUMP CRAB MEAT BEFORE SERVING.

❏ GARNISH WITH LEMON AND LIME WEDGES.

❏ PRESENTATION IN A MARTINI OR SUNDAE GLASS ADDS TO THE AMBIANCE OF THIS DISH.

THIS IS A GREAT PARTY DISH WITH A UNIQUE TASTE. FRESH CRABMEAT AND CHILI-LIME TORTILLA CHIPS ADD THE PIZZAZZ TO THESE EASY NACHOS. SHRIMP ALSO WORKS WELL WITH THIS RECIPE.

PREHEAT OVEN TO 350°

# CRAB NACHOS

(SERVES 6 - 8)

| | |
|---|---|
| 1 | LB. JUMBO, LUMP CRABMEAT (PICKED CLEAN) |
| 2 | CUPS CHEF JOE'S TOMATILLO SALSA (RECIPE ON PAGE 38) |
| 1 | CUP EXTRA-SHARP CHEDDAR CHEESE, GRATED |
| 1 | 9 OZ. BAG CHILI-LIME TORTILLA CHIPS OR ANY CHIPS OF YOUR CHOICE |

## PREPARATION

❑ PLACE CHIPS ON COOKIE SHEET AND HEAT IN THE OVEN FOR 4 MINUTES.

❑ WHILE CHIPS ARE HEATING, STIR 2 CUPS OF SALSA INTO SAUTÉ PAN OVER MEDIUM HEAT AND COOK UNTIL IT BEGINS TO BOIL.

❑ REMOVE SALSA FROM HEAT AND GENTLY FOLD IN CRABMEAT.

❑ TAKE TORTILLA CHIPS FROM OVEN AND SET TEMPERATURE TO BROIL.

❑ PLACE CHIPS IN AN OVEN-PROOF SERVING DISH OR PLATTER.

❑ SPOON HOT SALSA/CRABMEAT OVER CHIPS AND SPRINKLE WITH GRATED CHEESE.

❑ RETURN TO MIDDLE RACK IN OVEN AND BAKE UNTIL CHEESE BUBBLES.

❑ REMOVE AND SERVE IMMEDIATELY.

OPTION: SERVE THE NACHOS WITH SOUR CREAM, SLICED BLACK OLIVES, BLACK BEANS OR ANY OF YOUR FAVORITE NACHO TOPPINGS.

## GARLIC STONE CRAB CLAWS

(1 LB. PER PERSON)

FRESHLY CAUGHT STONE CRABS FROM THE GULF OF MEXICO ARE OUTSTANDING! ABSOLUTELY MY FAVORITE FOOD, I LIKE THEM ANY WAY THEY ARE PREPARED — HOT OR COLD, WITH MUSTARD SAUCE, BUTTER AND LEMON, ANY WAY AT ALL. I ADAPTED THE FOLLOWING RECIPE FROM A GARLIC, BLUE-CLAW CRAB DISH THAT I MAKE. YOU WILL WANT TO PREPARE ONE POUND OF STONE CRAB CLAWS PER PERSON.

| | |
|---|---|
| 1 | LB. OF FRESH STONE CRAB CLAWS, CRACKED (PER SERVING) |
| 2 | TBSP. LITE OLIVE OIL |
| 4 | LARGE GARLIC CLOVES, MINCED |
| 1/2 | STICK UNSALTED BUTTER |

JUICE OF 1 LEMON
PINCH OF CAYENNE PEPPER

MS. SYLVIA THOMPSON, MY FRIEND AND PATRON, LOVES STONE CRABS AS MUCH AS I DO!

### PREPARATION

❏ HEAT OLIVE OIL OVER MEDIUM-HIGH HEAT IN A LARGE PAN UNTIL HOT (BUT NOT SMOKING).
❏ ADD GARLIC AND STIR FOR ONE MINUTE, MAKING SURE IT DOESN'T BURN.
❏ ADD CRACKED STONE CRAB CLAWS AND BUTTER.
❏ TOSS AND TURN CLAWS, SOAKING UP GARLIC BUTTER INTO THE MEAT (ABOUT 2 MINUTES).
❏ STIR IN LEMON JUICE AND CAYENNE PEPPER.
❏ CONTINUE COOKING STONE CRAB CLAWS FOR 3 MORE MINUTES.
❏ SERVE IMMEDIATELY.

JESSIE DERHAM ANTICIPATES
A REPAST OF STONE CRABS BY
CANDLELIGHT ON LONGBOAT KEY.

MOST OF US LOVE A GOOD CRAB CAKE. I MAKE MANY
DIFFERENT KINDS OF CRAB CAKES, SOME PREPARED WITH
MASHED POTATOES AND CHIVES, OTHERS WITH MINCED
SHRIMP AND LOBSTER. THESE ARE THE "REAL McCOY,"
JUMBO LUMP CRAB CAKES THAT PLEASE EVERYONE'S TASTE.
THE JALAPEÑOS ADD JUST THE RIGHT KICK.

# JALAPEÑO CRAB CAKES

(SERVES 4)

| | |
|---|---|
| 1 | CUP FRESH BREAD CRUMBS |
| 1 | LB. FRESH JUMBO LUMP CRAB MEAT (PICKED CLEAN) |

## PREPARATION I

- ❑ SLICE PIECES OF WHITE BREAD AS FINE AS POSSIBLE.
- ❑ PLACE BREAD PIECES IN A BOWL.
- ❑ SPREAD CRAB MEAT OVER TOP OF BREAD.
- ❑ COVER AND REFRIGERATE FOR AT LEAST 1 HOUR.
- ❑ THE BREAD WILL SOAK UP THE JUICES OF THE CRAB MEAT.

| | |
|---|---|
| 1 | TBSP. HELLMANN'S MAYONNAISE |
| 1 | EXTRA LARGE EGG, BEATEN |
| 2 | TSP. DIJON MUSTARD |
| 1 | SCALLION, WHITE AND GREEN PARTS FINELY CHOPPED |
| 1/4 | CUP FRESH PARSLEY, CHOPPED |
| 2 | JALAPEÑO PEPPERS, SEEDED AND MINCED |
| 1/2 | TSP. DRY MUSTARD |
| 1 | TSP. HOT SAUCE |
| 1 | TSP. WORCESTERSHIRE SAUCE |
| 1 | TSP. OLD BAY SEASONING |
| 1/2 | TSP. KOSHER SALT |

JUICE OF 1/2 FRESH LEMON
DASH OF CAYENNE PEPPER
DASH OF WHITE PEPPER
CANOLA OIL FOR SAUTÉING
DRIED BREAD CRUMBS OR
CRACKER MEAL FOR COATING

(CONTINUES ON NEXT PAGE)

## JALAPEÑO CRAB CAKES

(CONTINUED)

### PREPARATION II

- ❏ PLACE INGREDIENTS IN A BOWL.
- ❏ STIR UNTIL BLENDED WELL.
- ❏ GENTLY FOLD CRAB AND BREAD CRUMBS INTO MIXTURE.
- ❏ FORM MIXTURE INTO CAKES OF A DESIRED SIZE: SMALL FOR APPETIZER, LARGE FOR ENTRÉE.
- ❏ COAT CRAB CAKES WITH DRIED BREAD CRUMBS OR CRACKER MEAL.
- ❏ PLACE IN REFRIGERATOR FOR AT LEAST 1 HOUR UNTIL THEY FIRM UP.
- ❏ HEAT ½ INCH OF CANOLA OIL IN SAUTÉ PAN OVER MEDIUM-HIGH HEAT (THE OIL SHOULD BE HOT BUT NOT SMOKING).
- ❏ ADD CRAB CAKES TO OIL AND COOK UNTIL GOLDEN BROWN (ABOUT 3 MINUTES PER SIDE), TURNING ONLY ONCE.
- ❏ REMOVE CRAB CAKES FROM PAN. DRAIN ON A PAPER TOWEL.
- ❏ SERVE WITH YOUR FAVORITE SEAFOOD SAUCE.

I'VE BEEN SERVING OYSTERS ROCKY FOR OVER 30 YEARS AND IT HAS ALWAYS BEEN A HIT. USE THE FRESHEST, LARGEST OYSTERS AVAILABLE. OPEN THEM CAREFULLY WITH AN OYSTER KNIFE. IF YOU ARE UNFAMILIAR WITH PRYING OPEN OYSTERS, ASK YOUR FISH SELLER TO DEMONSTRATE THE PROPER TECHNIQUE.

# OYSTERS ROCKY

(SERVES 2)

PREHEAT OVEN TO 450°

| | |
|---|---|
| 4 | CUPS FROZEN SPINACH, THAWED AND WELL DRAINED |
| 6 | LARGE GARLIC CLOVES, MINCED OR CRUSHED |
| 1 | LARGE SHALLOT, MINCED |
| 1 | CUP HEAVY CREAM |
| 6 | STRIPS OF BACON, COOKED CRISP AND DRAINED; RESERVE THE DRIPPINGS |
| 1/2 | CUP OF PERNOD LIQUOR |
| 1/4 | TSP. CAYENNE PEPPER |
| 1 | TSP. HOT SAUCE |
| 1 | TSP. KOSHER SALT |
| 1/2 | TSP. GROUND BLACK PEPPER |
| 12 | LARGE, OPENED OYSTERS ON THE HALF SHELL |

FRESH, GRATED PARMESAN CHEESE

## PREPARATION

- ❏ SAUTÉ GARLIC AND SHALLOTS IN THE BACON DRIPPINGS FOR 3 MINUTES.
- ❏ STIR IN SPINACH AND ADD HEAVY CREAM.
- ❏ BRING TO A BOIL AND TURN OFF HEAT.
- ❏ ADD PERNOD AND SPICES, BLENDING WELL.
- ❏ SPOON SPINACH MIXTURE OVER OYSTERS ON THE HALF SHELL.
- ❏ SPRINKLE LIBERALLY WITH PARMESAN CHEESE AND BAKE IN THE OVEN FOR 10-12 MINUTES.
- ❏ TOP WITH 1/2 SLICE OF BACON AND SERVE.

## GROUPER IN A BAG

(SERVES 1)

FRESHLY CAUGHT GROUPER IS MY MOST PREFERRED FISH TO COOK AND ENJOY. OF THE COUNTLESS WAYS THAT I HAVE PREPARED THIS FISH OVER THE YEARS, THIS RECIPE GIVES IT AN EXTRA BUMP THAT WILL IMPRESS YOUR GUESTS. THIS IS AN EZ AND FUN DISH TO MAKE; THE BEAUTY OF IT IS THAT IT CAN BE MADE AHEAD OF TIME AND THEN BAKED RIGHT BEFORE SERVING. THIS DISH GOES WELL WITH A SIDE OF PASTA TOSSED WITH OLIVE OIL, FRESH HERBS, GARLIC AND PARMESAN CHEESE.

PREHEAT OVEN TO 425°

1 FRESH GROUPER FILET 6 — 8 OUNCES
2 THICK SLICES OF FRESH RIPE TOMATO
3 LARGE FRESH BASIL LEAVES
2 THIN SLICES OF FLORIDA SWEET ONION OR RED ONION
1 YELLOW, RED AND GREEN PEPPER RING (ABOUT 1/4 INCH THICK)
2 WHITE MUSHROOMS, THINLY SLICED
2 LARGE GARLIC CLOVES SLICED AS THIN AS POSSIBLE
1 TBSP. LARGE CAPERS — NOT RINSED
1/4 CUP WHITE WINE
1 TSP. OLIVE OIL
1 TSP. CHOPPED ITALIAN PARSLEY
JUICE OF 1 FRESH LEMON
KOSHER SALT, BLACK PEPPER & OLIVE OIL FOR BRUSHING
12 BY 12 INCH PIECE OF PARCHMENT PAPER

### PREPARATION

❑ BRUSH ONE SIDE OF THE PARCHMENT PAPER WITH OLIVE OIL.
❑ JUICE THE LEMON ON BOTH SIDES OF THE GROUPER FILET, SEASON WITH SALT AND PEPPER AND PLACE ON OILED PAPER.
❑ OVERLAP THE TOMATO AND ONION ON TOP OF THE FILET AND PLACE A FRESH BASIL LEAF BETWEEN EACH SLICE.
❑ PLACE YOUR PEPPER RINGS OVER THE TOMATO AND ONION, ADD THE MUSHROOMS, GARLIC AND CAPERS.
❑ POUR ON THE WHITE WINE AND OLIVE OIL.
❑ SPRINKLE PARSLEY ON TOP ALONG WITH SALT AND PEPPER.
❑ FOLD UP THE PAPER OR FOIL, SEALING IT.
❑ PLACE THE "BAG" ON A SHEET PAN AND THEN INTO THE OVEN FOR 12 MINUTES.
❑ REMOVE AND SERVE WITH LEMON WEDGES.

BRENDA & BOB MITCHELL
HOST THE BEST EASTER EGG HUNT
AND BRUNCH IN TOWN.

Talk about a fast, EZ appetizer that's really good and different! Here's one that your guests will enjoy. In this recipe, I use an exceptionally flavorful product called "Makoto ginger dressing." This dressing is perfect for experimenting with and creating new dishes.

# GINGERED SCALLOPS

(SERVES 4)

| | |
|---|---|
| 1 | TBSP. OLIVE OIL |
| 1 | LB. FRESH SCALLOPS, DRAINED AND PATTED DRY |
| 1 | 8 OZ. CAN OF SLICED WATER CHESTNUTS, DRAINED |
| 1 | 8 OZ. BOTTLE MAKOTO GINGER DRESSING |
| 1 | 8 OZ. CAN OF PINEAPPLE CHUNKS (WITH JUICE) |

JUICE OF 1 LIME
SMALL WOODEN SKEWERS

## PREPARATION

❏ HEAT OLIVE OIL IN LARGE SKILLET OVER HIGH HEAT UNTIL VERY HOT (BUT NOT SMOKING).

❏ CAREFULLY ADD SCALLOPS AND SAUTÉ FOR ABOUT 3 MINUTES, STIRRING GENTLY.

❏ ADD LIME JUICE, WATER CHESTNUTS AND PINEAPPLE CHUNKS.

❏ STIR IN THE MAKOTO GINGER DRESSING AND MIX.

❏ BRING TO A BOIL, THEN REMOVE FROM HEAT.

❏ PRESENT SCALLOPS, WATER CHESTNUTS, AND PINEAPPLES WITH SKEWERS AND LET YOUR GUESTS SERVE THEMSELVES.

Fresh shrimp drizzled with lime, garlic and cilantro. Simple and delicious.

TURN OVEN TO BROIL

# Broiled Citrus Shrimp

(serves 6 - 8)

| | |
|---|---|
| 2 | LB. JUMBO SHRIMP, PEELED, DEVEINED, TAILS ON |
| 20 | LARGE GARLIC CLOVES |
| 1/2 | CUP WHITE WINE (CHARDONNAY OR CHABLIS) |
| 1 | STICK UNSALTED BUTTER |
| 1/2 | CUP FRESH CILANTRO, CHOPPED |
| 3 | JALAPEÑO PEPPERS, MINCED (SEEDS INCLUDED) |

JUICE OF 3 LIMES
KOSHER SALT
BLACK PEPPER

## PREPARATION

❑ PLACE GARLIC IN A SAUCEPAN AND COVER WITH WATER.
❑ BRING TO A BOIL OVER HIGH HEAT, THEN LOWER HEAT AND SIMMER FOR 20 MINUTES UNTIL GARLIC IS SOFT. REMOVE FROM SAUCEPAN. LET COOL. CHOP GARLIC FINE.
❑ PLACE SHRIMP IN A GLASS OR STAINLESS STEEL BOWL, ADD LIME JUICE.
❑ TOSS SHRIMP IN JUICE, THEN COVER AND REFRIGERATE.
❑ PLACE BUTTER IN SAUCEPAN AND MELT OVER LOW HEAT.

❑ ADD WHITE WINE TO BUTTER AND BRING TO A BOIL.
❑ REDUCE HEAT AND SIMMER FOR 3 MINUTES.
❑ STIR IN CILANTRO AND GARLIC, THEN REMOVE FROM HEAT.
❑ PLACE SHRIMP AND LIME JUICE IN A BAKING PAN, DISTRIBUTING SHRIMP EVENLY.
❑ SPOON BUTTER, GARLIC, CILANTRO AND WINE SAUCE OVER THE SHRIMP.
❑ SPRINKLE WITH KOSHER SALT.
❑ PLACE UNDER BROILER ON TOP RACK FOR 3 MINUTES. TURN SHRIMP OVER AND BROIL FOR AN ADDITIONAL 2 MINUTES.
❑ PLACE SHRIMP ON A SERVING PLATTER, SPRINKLE WITH CHOPPED JALAPEÑOS AND SERVE.

A BLEND OF FRESH SEAFOOD, CRUSTY BREAD AND GRUYERE
CHEESE GIVE THIS DISH A SCRUMPTIOUS TASTE.

PREHEAT OVEN TO 375°

# SEAFOOD BAGUETTES

(SERVES 2)

| 1 | LOAF OF CRUSTY, FRENCH BREAD |
| 4 | JUMBO SHRIMP, PEELED, DEVEINED, TAILS OFF |
| 4 | LARGE SEA SCALLOPS |
| 1 | 4 OZ. PIECE OF GROUPER (CUT INTO 2 INCH PIECES) |
| 1 | TBSP. CAPERS |
| 1 | 8 OZ. CAN OF CLAM JUICE |
| 1 | BAY LEAF |
| 1/2 | CUP WHITE WINE |
| 1/2 | TSP. DRIED TARRAGON |
| 1/2 | TSP. KOSHER SALT |
| 1 | TBSP. UNSALTED BUTTER |

2 OZ. GRATED GRUYERE CHEESE
4 OZ. LUMP CRABMEAT (PICKED CLEAN)
PINCH OF CAYENNE PEPPER
OLIVE OIL FOR BRUSHING BREAD

## PREPARATION

- ❑ SLICE BREAD INTO ROUNDS (1 INCH THICK). BRUSH BOTH SIDES WITH OLIVE OIL.
- ❑ PLACE ON A BAKING SHEET BRUSHED WITH OLIVE OIL. COOK AT 375° UNTIL BROWNED.
- ❑ REMOVE FROM OVEN AND ARRANGE ON SERVING PLATTER, OVERLAPPING THE SLICES.
- ❑ TURN OVEN TO BROIL.
- ❑ MIX WATER, WINE, BAY LEAF, TARRAGON, SALT AND CAYENNE PEPPER IN SAUCEPAN, THEN BRING TO A BOIL OVER MEDIUM-HIGH HEAT.
- ❑ REDUCE HEAT TO SIMMER. ADD SHRIMP, SCALLOPS AND FISH.
- ❑ STIR GENTLY AND COVER WITH THE LID.
- ❑ LET SEAFOOD POACH FOR 3 MINUTES.
- ❑ REMOVE AND DISTRIBUTE OVER BREAD ROUNDS.
- ❑ TOP WITH LUMP CRABMEAT AND SPRINKLE WITH SHREDDED GRUYERE CHEESE.
- ❑ RETURN TO OVEN AND BROIL ON MIDDLE OVEN RACK UNTIL CHEESE BROWNS LIGHTLY.
- ❑ STIR BUTTER INTO POACHING BROTH.
- ❑ DRIZZLE BROTH OVER SANDWICHES.
- ❑ TOP WITH CAPERS, SERVE WITH LEMON WEDGES.

IF YOU LIKE SUSHI, YOU WILL LOVE THIS. I SERVE THE TUNA WITH WASABI, PICKLED GINGER, CUCUMBER AND CELLOPHANE NOODLES. IT'S A BIG HIT!

# RARE TUNA PLATTER

(SERVES 4)

I LOVE CATERING FOR TAMMY PARROTT & VALERIE CROW. THEIR PARTIES ARE SPECTACULAR.

CANOLA OIL FOR SAUTÉING

| | |
|---|---|
| 1 | LB. PIECE OF SUSHI-GRADE TUNA, TRIMMED |
| 1 | TSP. GROUND BLACK PEPPER |
| 1/2 | PACK CELLOPHANE NOODLES (2 OZ. DRY) |
| 4 | CUPS BOILING WATER |
| 1 | CUCUMBER CUT INTO 2 PIECES (3 INCHES EACH) |
| 2 | OZ. PICKLED GINGER |
| 2 | OZ. WASABI |
| 2 | TBSP. SOY SAUCE |
| 1 | TSP. KOSHER SALT |

## PREPARATION

❑ COAT TUNA WITH PEPPER.
❑ HEAT CANOLA OIL IN A NON-STICK FRYING PAN UNTIL VERY HOT (ALMOST SMOKING).
❑ CAREFULLY PLACE TUNA IN HOT PAN, QUICKLY SEARING BOTH SIDES.
❑ REMOVE AND SET ON PAPER TOWEL TO DRAIN.
❑ PLACE CELLOPHANE NOODLES IN BOWL AND COVER WITH WATER AND SALT.
❑ LET SIT FOR 15 MINUTES, THEN DRAIN AND SET ASIDE.
❑ TOSS NOODLES WITH SOY SAUCE AND CENTER ON SERVING PLATTER.
❑ HOLLOW OUT CUCUMBER PIECES, FILL WITH WASABI.
❑ PLACE CUCUMBERS ON A BED OF GINGER AT EITHER SIDE OF THE PLATE.
❑ SLICE TUNA AS THIN AS POSSIBLE AND LAYER AROUND NOODLES.
❑ SPRINKLE ENTIRE PLATTER WITH SESAME SEEDS.

JASMINE BREWER, OUR BEAUTIFUL MERMAID
FROM STAR FISH CO. IN CORTEZ VILLAGE.

THE WHOLE FISH ON THE LEFT PAGE IS A 2.5 POUND MANGROVE SNAPPER CAUGHT IN THE WATERS OFF OF CORTEZ (FL). THE QUANTITY OF INGREDIENTS YOU WILL USE FOR THE STUFFING WILL DEPEND ON THE SIZE OF THE FISH. YOU WILL NEED TO ADJUST THE RECIPE TO ACCOMMODATE THE SIZE OF THE FISH YOU ARE USING. FOR A 2 - 3 POUND FISH, FOLLOW THE RECIPE BELOW.

# GRILLED WHOLE STUFFED FISH

(SERVES 2 - 4)

PREHEAT GRILL TO HIGH

| | |
|---|---|
| 1 | WHOLE FISH, (SNAPPER, GROUPER OR THE FISH OF YOUR CHOICE) |
| 1 | BUNCH FRESH ITALIAN PARSLEY, CHOPPED COARSELY |
| 1 | LARGE BULB FENNEL, CHOPPED INTO 2 INCH PIECES |
| 3 | BAY LEAVES |
| 1 | WHOLE SHALLOT, MINCED |
| 1 | TBSP. RED PEPPER FLAKES |
| 2 | FRESH ORANGES WITH SKINS ON (SLICED INTO QUARTERS) |

KOSHER SALT
BLACK PEPPER
EXTRA VIRGIN OLIVE OIL

## PREPARATION

❑ HAVE FISH CLEANED, SCALED AND GUTTED (GILLS AND FINS REMOVED AT THE FISH MARKET). THIS PROCESS WILL LEAVE THE FISH SPLIT WITH A CAVITY FOR STUFFING.

❑ RUB SKIN AND INSIDE OF FISH WITH A COATING OF OLIVE OIL, KOSHER SALT AND BLACK PEPPER.

❑ COMBINE REMAINING INGREDIENTS IN A LARGE BOWL AND MIX TOGETHER.

❑ DISTRIBUTE INGREDIENTS EVENLY THROUGH FISH CAVITY AND CLOSE.

❑ PLACE FISH ONTO HOT GRILL, THEN LOWER HEAT TO MEDIUM.

❑ IF USING A CHARCOAL GRILL, MOVE FISH TOWARD THE OUTSIDE WHERE IT IS LESS HOT.

(CONTINUES ON NEXT PAGE)

## GRILLED WHOLE STUFFED FISH
(CONTINUED)

❑ COOKING TIME DEPENDS ON THE SIZE AND TYPE OF FISH YOU ARE USING. JUST REMEMBER THAT COOKING ON TOO HIGH A HEAT WILL BURN THE OUTSIDE AND LEAVE THE INSIDE UNDERCOOKED. LET FISH SIT LONG ENOUGH TO COOK THROUGH ON ONE SIDE, THEN TURN IT. WHEN THE THICKEST PART OF THE FLESH NEAR THE BONE FLAKES WHEN PRODDED BY A FORK, THE FISH IS DONE.
❑ PEEL OFF SKIN.
❑ PLACE WHOLE FISH ON A LARGE PLATTER WITH SOME LEMON WEDGES AND A LOT OF MIXED, GRILLED VEGETABLES LIKE EGGPLANT, YELLOW SQUASH, ZUCCHINI, MUSHROOMS, RED AND GREEN PEPPERS, RED ONIONS, ETC., ALONG WITH FRESH FENNEL AND ORANGES.

## BBQ ALASKAN SALMON

(SERVES 4 - 6)

BBQ ALASKAN SALMON
THIS IS A SPECTACULAR DISH WITH GREAT FLAVORS AND TASTE. THROUGHOUT ALASKA THEY HAVE COOKOUTS CALLED "SALMON BAKES." FRESHLY CAUGHT ALASKAN SALMON ARE MARINATED, GRILLED AND THEN SAUCED, WITH EACH COOK TRYING TO OUTDO THE OTHER. I THINK I HAVE OUTDONE MYSELF WITH THIS ONE. GIVE IT A TRY. IT'S FUN TO DO AND A GREAT WAY TO PREPARE SALMON!

PREHEAT GRILL TO HIGH

1 SIDE OF FRESH SALMON, ABOUT 2 LBS., WITH BONES REMOVED AND SKIN LEFT ON

MARINADE
2 TBSP. LITE SOY SAUCE
1 TSP. KOSHER SALT
1 TSP. HOT SAUCE
1 CUP WHITE WINE
2 TBSP. MINCED FRESH GINGER (PEELED GINGER)
1/4 CUP HONEY
1/2 TSP. CAYENNE PEPPER
JUICE OF 2 LEMONS

(CONTINUES ON PAGE 34)

## BBQ
## ALASKAN
## SALMON
(CONTINUED)

### PREPARATION

- ❑ MIX MARINADE INGREDIENTS IN A BOWL.
- ❑ PLACE SALMON (SKIN SIDE DOWN) IN A GLASS OR STAINLESS STEEL BAKING PAN.
- ❑ POUR MARINADE OVER FISH.
- ❑ COVER WITH FILM WRAP AND REFRIGERATE FOR AT LEAST AN HOUR, TURNING SEVERAL TIMES TO INSURE SATURATION AND EVEN DISTRIBUTION.

### SALMON SAUCE

| 1 | STICK UNSALTED BUTTER |
| 1/2 | CUP PACKED BROWN SUGAR |
| 1 | CUP WHITE WINE (CHARDONNAY OR CHABLIS) |
| 4 | LARGE GARLIC CLOVES, MINCED OR CRUSHED |
| 2 | SCALLIONS (CHOPPED) |
| 1 | TSP. KOSHER SALT |
| 1/4 | TSP. CAYENNE PEPPER |

JUICE OF 2 LEMONS

### PREPARATION

- ❑ PLACE BUTTER IN SAUCEPAN AND COOK UNTIL IT BUBBLES (OVER LOW HEAT).
- ❑ ADD BROWN SUGAR TO BUTTER AND STIR, COOKING FOR ABOUT 2 MINUTES.
- ❑ STIR IN OTHER INGREDIENTS AND SIMMER FOR 5 MINUTES. REMOVE FROM HEAT AND SET ASIDE.
- ❑ TAKE SALMON FROM MARINADE AND PLACE ON THE ALREADY HEATED GRILL (FLESH SIDE DOWN).
- ❑ COOK APPROXIMATELY 5 MINUTES.
- ❑ USING TWO SPATULAS, TURN FISH OVER AND COOK FOR ANOTHER 4 MINUTES.
- ❑ GENTLY PROD THICKEST PART OF FISH TO CHECK FOR DONENESS.
- ❑ CAREFULLY REMOVE FISH FROM GRILL. THE SKIN SHOULD STICK TO THE GRATING.
- ❑ PLACE ON A SERVING PLATTER, TOP WITH THE SAUCE AND SERVE WITH LEMON, LIME WEDGES AND GRILLED VEGETABLES.

Need a quick appetizer or entrée? This is it. The mango works exceptionally well with the seasoned shrimp. Try to use ripe, juicy mangoes. The hot shrimp will absorb the sweet nectar of this flavorful fruit.

| | |
|---|---|
| 1 | LB. JUMBO SHRIMP, PEEL AND DEVEIN, TAILS ON |
| 1/2 | CUP OLIVE OIL |
| 2 | JALAPEÑO PEPPERS, MINCED (SEEDS INCLUDED) |
| 2 | TBSP. CILANTRO, CHOPPED |
| 2 | TBSP. FRESH MINT, CHOPPED |
| 1 | TBSP. FRESH, PEELED GINGER, MINCED |
| 1 | TSP. KOSHER SALT |
| 1/2 | TSP. GROUND BLACK PEPPER |
| 1 | LARGE, RIPE, JUICY MANGO |

## GRILLED SHRIMP WITH FRESH MANGO

(APPETIZER: SERVES 4

ENTRÉE: SERVES 2)

Bobby and Bert Woodson in front of their famous seafood grille in Bradenton, Florida.

## PREPARATION

❑ Mix olive oil, jalapeños, cilantro, mint, ginger, kosher salt and pepper together.
❑ Add shrimp and toss.
❑ Cover and refrigerate for at least 1 hour.
❑ Pre-heat grill to high.
❑ Peel and slice fresh mango into bite-sized pieces.
❑ Remove shrimp from marinade and set aside.
❑ Place marinade in a saucepan and bring to a boil.
❑ Reduce range heat to low and simmer for 3 minutes.
❑ Lower grill heat to medium-high.
❑ Place shrimp on grill.
❑ Cook for about 2 - 3 minutes on each side, turning only once.
❑ Remove shrimp from grill and serve on a platter. Top with fresh mango.
❑ Pour cooked marinade over shrimp and mango.

The heat of the jalapeños, the fragrance of the cilantro, mint, and ginger combined with the sweetness of the mango truly accentuates the flavor of this shrimp dish.

37

## A Toast (Skål)

BY GEORGE PETER RYAN, LIDO KEY, FLORIDA

THE VIKINGS HAD AN INTERESTING USE FOR A TOAST. THEY WERE KNOWN TO BE BARBARIANS WHO FOUND IT BEST NOT TO TRUST THEIR OWN KIND. VIKING LEADERS WOULD SECURE ALLIANCES BY FILLING THEIR DRINKING-HORNS WITH MJØD (SAY MEURD), A FAVORED DRINK AND CLASH THEM TOGETHER WITH ENOUGH FORCE TO MIX THE LIQUID FROM EACH HORN. BY THIS MIXING OF DRINKS, THE VIKING LEADERS COULD BE REASONABLY ASSURED THE MJØD HAD NOT BEEN SPIKED WITH A LESS THAN OBVIOUS DEADLY WEAPON.

(BOTTOM RIGHT PHOTO)
AFTER A DAY OF COOKING,
CHEF JOE TOASTS THE VIKINGS:
TROND RAMBERG,
PETER ANDERSEN AND THE LOVELY
LE THUY THI NGUYEN.

MANY THANKS!

*HAIL RAGNAR!*

Fresh, ripe avocados are essential to the success of this quick appetizer. I use the green Florida avocado, but the California "Haas" variety is also good.

| | |
|---|---|
| 2 | ripe avocados |
| 1 | ripe tomato (medium), finely chopped |
| 1 | small jalapeño, seeded and minced |
| 1/2 | medium onion, minced |
| 2 | garlic cloves, minced |
| 1 | 4 oz. can mild green chilies, drained and chopped |
| 1 | tsp. kosher salt |

juice of 1 fresh lime

# Chef Joe's EZ Guacamole

(4 cups)

## PREPARATION

❏ Cut avocados in half, discard seeds and remove pulp from skin.

❏ Place pulp, lime juice, and salt in a bowl and thoroughly mash with fork.

❏ Fold tomatoes, onion, garlic, chilies and jalapeños into the mashed avocado.

❏ Serve with chips or vegetables.

# TOMATILLO SALSA

ACCORDING TO YOUR TASTE, YOU CAN TURN UP THE HEAT IN THIS RECIPE BY ADDING EXTRA PEPPERS SUCH AS HABANERO OR DRIED CHILIES.

(6 CUPS)

## INGREDIENTS

| | |
|---|---|
| 1 | SMALL RED ONION, CHOPPED |
| 1 | GREEN PEPPER, CHOPPED |
| 2 | CLOVES GARLIC, MINCED |
| 1/4 | CUP FRESH PARSLEY, CHOPPED |
| 1/4 | CUP FRESH CILANTRO, CHOPPED |
| 2 | FRESH JALAPEÑO PEPPERS, SEEDED AND MINCED |
| 4 | RIPE TOMATOES, CHOPPED |
| 2 | MEDIUM TOMATILLOS (MEXICAN TOMATOES), HUSKED AND CHOPPED |
| 1 | TSP. KOSHER SALT |
| 1 | TSP. CUMIN |
| 1 | TSP. CHILI POWDER |
| 1/2 | TSP. CHILI PEPPER FLAKES |
| 1/4 | TSP. BLACK PEPPER |
| 1/2 | CUP OLIVE OIL |
| 1/4 | CUP RED WINE VINEGAR |

JUICE OF 1 LIME
GOOD PINCH OF WHITE PEPPER
GOOD PINCH CAYENNE PEPPER

## PREPARATION

MIX ALL INGREDIENTS TOGETHER AND REFRIGERATE. SERVE WITH CHIPS.

### VARIATIONS

ADD YOUR CHOICE OF MANGO, PINEAPPLE, WATERMELON, AVOCADO, PEACH, OR ANY COMBINATION OF THESE INGREDIENTS TO THE TOMATILLO SALSA. YOU CAN USE SALSA TO TASTEFULLY ACCENT GRILLED MEATS OR SEAFOOD.

By far, my most requested salad dressing, This caesar is extremely easy to make. Use the freshest ingredients available, especially the parmesan cheese. This refrigerates well.

# Caesar Salad Dressing

(6 cups)

| | |
|---|---|
| 12 | LARGE CLOVES OF FRESH GARLIC |
| 1 | 2 OZ. CAN OF ANCHOVY FILLETS (WITH OIL) |
| 3 | TBSP. DIJON MUSTARD |
| 2 | TSP. DRY MUSTARD |
| 3/4 | CUP RED WINE VINEGAR |
| 3 | CUPS HELLMANN'S MAYONNAISE |
| 1/2 | CUP FRESH PARSLEY, CHOPPED |
| 1 | TBSP. WORCESTERSHIRE SAUCE |
| 1 | TSP. BLACK PEPPER |
| 1/4 | CUP FRESH LEMON JUICE |
| 3 | PACKED CUPS OF FRESHLY GRATED PARMESAN CHEESE |
| 2 | DASHES OF CAYENNE PEPPER |

## PREPARATION

❏ Place all ingredients in food processor.
❏ Use the "pulsing force" to grind down ingredients and then blend until smooth.
❏ Toss desired amount of dressing with crisp, cold romaine lettuce and croutons.

I've made a habit of saving leftover french bread pieces and freezing them. When I make caesar salad, I just defrost the bread, cut it into crouton-size pieces, drizzle with olive oil and bake in the oven until lightly browned.

THIS SALAD IS CRUNCHY, SOFT, SWEET, SOUR, HOT AND COLD ALL AT THE SAME TIME. PREPARE THE INGREDIENTS IN A LARGE BOWL, LAYERING EVERYTHING ACCORDING TO THE LIST BELOW, WITH SPINACH AS THE FIRST INGREDIENT ON THE BOTTOM. BRING THE SPINACH UP FROM THE BOTTOM AND TOSS LIGHTLY WITH TONGS BEFORE SERVING, WITH THE HOT DRESSING ON THE SIDE.

## FRESH SPINACH SALAD WITH HOT POPPY SEED DRESSING

(SERVES 8)

| | |
|---|---|
| 1 | LARGE 10 OZ. BAG OF FRESH SPINACH LEAVES, WASHED, DRIED AND STEMMED |
| 1 | MEDIUM RED ONION, THINLY SLICED INTO RINGS |
| 8 | OZ. FRESH WHITE MUSHROOMS, WASHED & THINLY SLICED |
| 8 | OZ. GRAPE TOMATOES, HALVED |
| 2 | FRESH ORANGES, PEELED AND CUT INTO RINGS |
| 2 | CUPS OF CHOPPED WALNUTS OR PECANS |
| 4 | HARD BOILED EGGS, CUT INTO QUARTERS |
| 8 | OZ. OF CRISPLY COOKED BACON (1 INCH PIECES) |

HOT POPPY SEED DRESSING

| | |
|---|---|
| 2 | TBSP. BACON DRIPPINGS OR CANOLA OIL |
| 1 | LARGE CLOVE OF GARLIC, MINCED OR CRUSHED |
| 1 | LARGE TOMATO, FINELY CHOPPED |
| 2 | SCALLIONS, MINCED |
| 2 | BAY LEAVES |
| 3/4 | CUP RED WINE VINEGAR |
| 1 1/2 | CUPS WATER |
| 1 | 9 OZ. BOTTLE OF CROSSE & BLACKWELL'S HOT MANGO CHUTNEY |
| 2 | TSP. CURRY POWDER |
| 2 | TSP. POPPY SEEDS |
| 1 | TSP. KOSHER SALT |
| 1/2 | TSP. GROUND BLACK PEPPER |

DASH OF CAYENNE PEPPER

## PREPARATION
❑ HEAT BACON DRIPPINGS OR CANOLA OIL IN A SMALL SAUCE PAN.
❑ ADD GARLIC AND SCALLIONS, AND SAUTÉ FOR 2 MINUTES.
❑ ADD TOMATOES AND BAY LEAVES, AND SAUTÉ FOR 3 MORE MINUTES.
❑ ADD REMAINING INGREDIENTS AND BRING TO A BOIL.
❑ REDUCE HEAT AND SIMMER 5 MINUTES.
❑ REMOVE BAY LEAVES AND SERVE HOT.

THE FRESH, RIPE, RED AND YELLOW TOMATOES CONTRAST BEAUTIFULLY WITH THE BUFFALO MOZZARELLA. NOT ONLY DOES THIS DISH TASTE GOOD, IT LOOKS GOOD. SOME OF THE BEST TOMATOES GROWN IN THE REGION COME FROM GERALDSON´S BARN IN MANATEE COUNTY, FLORIDA. REFRIGERATE DRESSING FOR AN HOUR BEFORE SERVING.

# SALAD FLORIDÈ

(SERVES 2)

| | |
|---|---|
| 1 | LARGE RIPE, YELLOW TOMATO, SLICED |
| 1 | LARGE RIPE, RED TOMATO, SLICED |
| 1 | SMALL RED ONION, SLICED THINLY INTO RINGS AND CUT IN HALF |
| 1 | MEDIUM BALL OF FRESH BUFFALO MOZZARELLA, SLICED THINLY |
| 4 | LARGE FRESH BASIL LEAVES, TORN INTO SMALL PIECES |
| 1 | TBSP. CAPERS, RINSED |

RED WINE VINEGAR
EXTRA VIRGIN OLIVE OIL
KOSHER SALT
GROUND BLACK PEPPER

LOUISE FOGARTY ENJOYS A GLASS OF WINE BEFORE DINNER. SALAD FLORIDÈ WILL BE THE FIRST COURSE.

## PREPARATION

❏ LAYER TOMATOES WITH COLORS OVERLAPPING ON A SERVING PLATTER.
❏ SPREAD RED ONION OVER TOMATOES.
❏ TOP WITH BUFFALO MOZZARELLA AND CAPERS.
❏ SPLASH WITH VINEGAR AND OLIVE OIL.
❏ SPRINKLE WITH SALT AND PEPPER.
❏ SERVE IMMEDIATELY.

Soups, bisques, chowders, whatever you call them -- we all love them. Bowls brimming with healthy, flavorful ingredients seasoned to our particular tastes. Here are a few of my patrons´ favorites.

# GAZPACHO
## Spanish Tomato & Vegetable Soup

## SERVE COLD

(SERVES 8-10)

| | |
|---|---|
| 1 | VIDALIA OR FLORIDA SWEET ONION, DICED |
| 2 | FIRM CUCUMBERS, PEELED, SEEDED AND DICED |
| 2 | PEPPERS, 1 RED AND 1 GREEN, SEEDED AND DICED |
| 6 | FRESH LARGE, RIPE TOMATOES, PEELED AND DICED |
| 2 | FRESH JALAPEÑO PEPPERS, SEEDED AND MINCED |
| 6 | LARGE GARLIC CLOVES, MINCED OR CRUSHED |
| 1 | TSP. CUMIN |
| 1 | TSP. CHILI POWDER |
| 1/2 | CUP LITE OLIVE OIL |
| 1/2 | TSP. RED PEPPER FLAKES |
| 1 | TBSP. KOSHER SALT |
| 1/4 | CUP RED WINE VINEGAR |
| 1 | 48 OZ. CAN OF TOMATO JUICE |
| 2 | CUPS BEEF STOCK, BEEF BROTH OR CONSOMMÉ (IF MAKING VEGETARIAN STYLE, REPLACE BEEF STOCK WITH TOMATO JUICE) |

JUICE OF 2 FRESH LIMES
FRESH PARSLEY AND CILANTRO
    (CHOPPED FOR GARNISH)

## PREPARATION
❑ PLACE ALL INGREDIENTS IN A STAINLESS STEEL BOWL.
❑ BLEND TOGETHER AND CHILL.
❑ SERVE COLD. GARNISH WITH CHOPPED PARSLEY AND CILANTRO.

## Mushroom Bisque with Fresh Oysters
(SERVES 4)

HERE WE HAVE A DISH FIT FOR ROYALTY. THE SAVOURY OYSTERS ADD THE "CROWNING" TOUCH.

*CAREFUL - WHEN TRANSFERRING HOT LIQUIDS FROM A POT TO A PROCESSOR OR BLENDER, MAKE SURE THEY ARE COOL ENOUGH TO HANDLE.

| | |
|---|---|
| 1 | STICK OF UNSALTED BUTTER |
| 1 | LB. FRESH MUSHROOMS, WASHED AND SLICED |
| 1 | CUP CHOPPED ONIONS |
| 1 | TSP. DRIED THYME |
| 3/4 | CUP ALL-PURPOSE FLOUR |
| 8 | CUPS CHICKEN OR VEGETABLE STOCK, HEATED TO A BOIL |
| 1 | PINT HEAVY CREAM |
| 1 | CUP SHERRY |
| 16 | OYSTERS (4 PER SERVING) |

SALT AND PEPPER TO TASTE

## PREPARATION

- ❏ Melt butter in a large soup pot over medium heat.
- ❏ Cook until butter begins to bubble.
- ❏ Add mushrooms and onions. Cook 5 minutes, stirring occasionally.
- ❏ Add thyme and flour. Cook and stir.

- ❏ Cook and stir 3 more minutes until flour is absorbed.
- ❏ Slowly add hot stock and stir until it comes to a boil.
- ❏ Reduce heat to low and simmer for 60 minutes.
- ❏ Stir in heavy cream and bring to a boil again.
- ❏ Remove from heat.
- ❏ Add sherry, salt and pepper to taste.
- ❏ Let bisque sit until cool, then puree in a processor or blender.
- ❏ At serving time reheat bisque, bring to a boil.
- ❏ Pour hot into 4 serving bowls.
- ❏ For each bowl, place 4 shucked oysters on top.

ENJOYING VICHYSSOISE
WITH THE EVANS CLAN!

## VICHYSSOISE
### CHEF JOE'S FAMOUS LEEK & POTATO SOUP

**SERVE HOT OR COLD**

(4 - 6 SERVINGS)

A DELICATE, VELVET TEXTURED COMBINATION THAT IS DELICIOUS SERVED HOT OR COLD.

3    CUPS OF PEELED AND SLICED POTATOES (IDAHO OR RUSSET)
3    CUPS SLICED LEEKS (WHITE PART ONLY)
6    CUPS CHICKEN OR VEGETABLE STOCK
1    CUP HEAVY CREAM
SALT & PEPPER TO TASTE
FRESH CHIVES, MINCED FOR GARNISH

### PREPARATION

❑ BRING STOCK TO A BOIL. ADD POTATOES AND LEEKS, THEN REDUCE HEAT TO A SIMMER.
❑ COOK UNTIL POTATOES ARE SOFT.
❑ REMOVE FROM HEAT AND LET COOL.
❑ PURÉE SOUP IN A FOOD PROCESSOR OR BLENDER.
❑ RETURN SOUP TO THE POT AND ADD HEAVY CREAM.
❑ BRING BACK TO A BOIL, THEN REMOVE FROM HEAT.
❑ REFRIGERATE SOUP BEFORE SERVING IF YOU WOULD LIKE IT COLD.
❑ SEASON WITH SALT AND PEPPER. GARNISH WITH MINCED CHIVES AND SERVE.

FRESH ORANGE JUICE ADDS A NICE TOUCH TO AN ALREADY
DELICIOUS SOUP.

| | |
|---|---|
| 6 | LARGE RIPE TOMATOES, CHOPPED |
| 1 | ONION, CHOPPED |
| 2 | CARROTS, PEELED AND GRATED |
| 1 | GREEN PEPPER, SEEDED AND CHOPPED |
| 10 | FRESH BASIL LEAVES, CHOPPED |
| 6 | CUPS OF CHICKEN OR VEGETABLE STOCK |
| 1 | LARGE ZUCCHINI (WITH SKIN), GRATED |
| 2 | CUPS HEAVY CREAM |
| 1 | CUP FRESH ORANGE JUICE |

SALT & PEPPER TO TASTE
FRESHLY GRATED ORANGE RIND FOR GARNISH

## PREPARATION
- ❑ SET ASIDE GRATED ZUCCHINI, CREAM, AND ORANGE JUICE.
- ❑ PUT REMAINING INGREDIENTS IN A POT.  BRING TO A BOIL.
- ❑ REDUCE TO A SIMMER AND COOK FOR 15 MINUTES.
- ❑ PURÉE MIXTURE IN A FOOD PROCESSOR OR BLENDER.
- ❑ BRING MIXTURE BACK TO BOIL, THEN REDUCE TO SIMMER.
- ❑ STIR ZUCCHINI AND HEAVY CREAM INTO BISQUE.
  BRING TO A BOIL.
- ❑ REMOVE FROM HEAT, STIR ORANGE JUICE INTO SOUP.
- ❑ SERVE BISQUE HOT WITH GRATED ORANGE RIND.

# TOMATO &
# ZUCCHINI
# BISQUE

## SERVE HOT

(SERVES 10)

"COACH"
FRANK CAVANAUGH
PICKS A FRESH ORANGE
FOR THE BISQUE.

# VEGETABLE & CHICKEN STOCK

Butcher Doug Stivers', "Chop Shop" is a cut above the rest.

## VEGETABLE STOCK

| | |
|---|---|
| 2 | GREEN PEPPERS, SEEDED AND CHOPPED |
| 5 | ONIONS, CHOPPED |
| 3 | LEEKS, CHOPPED |
| 1 | BUNCH CELERY, CHOPPED (INCLUDING LEAVES) |
| 1 | BUNCH PARSLEY, CHOPPED |
| 6 | BAY LEAVES |
| 2 | TSP. DRIED MARJORAM |
| 2 | TSP. DRIED THYME |
| 2 | TBSP. WHOLE PEPPERCORNS |
| 2 | GALLONS OF COLD WATER |

### PREPARATION

❑ BRING ALL INGREDIENTS TO A BOIL. REDUCE HEAT AND SIMMER, SKIMMING OFF ANY FOAM THAT COMES TO THE TOP.

❑ COOK UNTIL STOCK REDUCES TO HALF (DO NOT STIR).

❑ LET STOCK COOL, THEN STRAIN THROUGH CHEESECLOTH OR FINE MESH STRAINER.

❑ REFRIGERATE OR FREEZE UNTIL NEEDED.

## CHICKEN STOCK

| | |
|---|---|
| 1 | WHOLE CHICKEN, WASHED IN COLD WATER |
| 2 | ONIONS, PEELED AND CHOPPED |
| 4 | CARROTS, PEELED AND CHOPPED |
| 4 | CELERY STRIPS, PEELED AND CHOPPED |
| 6 | CLOVES FRESH GARLIC, CHOPPED |
| 4 | BAY LEAVES |
| 1 | TBSP. DRIED THYME |
| 2 | TBSP. WHOLE PEPPERCORNS |

### PREPARATION

❑ COMBINE ALL INGREDIENTS IN A LARGE POT AND COVER WITH COLD WATER.

❑ BRING STOCK TO A BOIL AND THEN REDUCE TO A SIMMER.

❑ COOK UNTIL REDUCED TO HALF.

❑ STRAIN STOCK, REFRIGERATE.

❑ BE SURE TO REMOVE PEPPERCORNS FROM CHICKEN MEAT BEFORE SERVING.

HERE I AM WITH FARMER ERIC GERALDSON AT THE BARN.
GREAT RECIPES REQUIRE GREAT PRODUCTS.

## BEEF STOCK

| | |
|---|---|
| 6 | CARROTS, PEELED AND CHOPPED |
| 2 | ONIONS, PEELED AND CHOPPED |
| 6 | CELERY STALKS, CHOPPED |
| 6 | BAY LEAVES |
| 1 | BUNCH OF PARSLEY, CHOPPED |
| 2 | TBSP. WHOLE PEPPERCORNS |

6 TO 7 LBS. BEEF BONES

# BEEF STOCK

PREHEAT OVEN TO 425°

## PREPARATION

❑ PLACE BEEF BONES IN A ROASTING PAN. ROAST IN HOT OVEN (425°) FOR 60 MINUTES, TURNING AS NEEDED TO BROWN EVENLY (BE CAREFUL NOT TO BURN).

❑ ADD VEGETABLES TO PAN WITH BONES AND ROAST FOR ANOTHER 20 MINUTES.

❑ REMOVE FROM OVEN AND PLACE IN A LARGE POT. COVER WITH COOL WATER.

❑ ADD BAY LEAVES, PARSLEY AND PEPPER CORNS TO THE POT AND BRING TO A BOIL.

❑ REDUCE HEAT TO SIMMER.

❑ COOK UNTIL REDUCED TO HALF. LET COOL, THEN STRAIN.

❑ SKIM ANY FAT OFF THE TOP.

❑ REFRIGERATE OR FREEZE UNTIL NEEDED.

I FIRST MADE THIS DISH ON A WHI
USING SOME "CRUSTED PORK LO
NIGHT BEFORE, I TRIED MY HAND
"BANH MI." "BANH MI" TRANSLAT
REFERRING TO THE CRUSTY FREN
VARIOUS FOOD COMBINATIONS. I
VIETNAMESE BANH MI. THE SLAW
NICE TEXTURE AND A GREAT TAST

| | |
|---|---|
| 1 | LB. CRUSTED PORK LOIN, |
| 1/4 | CUP HOISIN SAUCE |
| 1/4 | CUP WATER |
| 1 | TBSP. FRESH GINGER, PEE |
| | MINCED |
| 2 | TBSP. FRESH CILANTRO, C |
| 1 | JALAPEÑO, SEEDED AND N |
| 4 | CRUSTY FRENCH ROLLS (● |

JUICE OF 1 LIME

## PREPARATION

❑ MIX SOY SAUCE, HOISIN SAUCE
AND GINGER IN A SMALL SAUTE
❑ BRING TO A BOIL AND ADD POF
❑ REDUCE HEAT TO SIMMER.
❑ STIR PORK THROUGH SAUCE, C
COATING EACH PIECE.
❑ ADD CILANTRO AND LIME JUICI
❑ PORTION OUT 4 SERVINGS ANI
ON THE ROLLS. TOP WITH ZES

ZESTY SLAW

| | |
|---|---|
| 4 | CUPS NAPA CABBAGE, FIN |
| 2 | LARGE CARROTS, SHREDD |
| 2 | SCALLIONS, CHOPPED |
| 1/2 | CUP LITE OLIVE OIL |
| 1/4 | CUP RICE VINEGAR |
| 1 | TSP. SUGAR |
| 2 | TBSP. CHOPPED FRESH MI |
| 2 | TSP. LITE SOY SAUCE |
| 1/4 | TSP. GROUND BLACK PEPF |

JUICE OF 2 LIMES

## PREPARATION          EZ - EZ - E

❑ TOSS INGREDIENTS AND MIX TH

(SERVES 6)

## INGREDIENTS

- 4 CUPS DRIED BLACK BEANS
- ¼ CUP OLIVE OIL
- 1 CUP ONION, CHOPPED
- 1 CUP GREEN PEPPER, CHOPPED
- ½ CUP RED PEPPER, CHOPPED
- 1 LARGE CARROT, GRATED
- 1 CELERY STRIP, CHOPPED
- 6 LARGE GARLIC CLOVES MINCED OR CRUSHED
- 2 SMOKED HAM HOCKS (OPTIONAL)
- ½ CUP FRESH PARSLEY, CHOPPED
- 1 TSP. DRIED BASIL
- 2 BAY LEAVES
- 1 TSP. DRIED OREGANO
- ½ TSP. DRIED THYME
- 1 TSP. CHILI PEPPER FLAKES
- 1 TBSP. KOSHER SALT
- 1 TBSP. CELERY SEED
- 1 TSP. BLACK PEPPER
- ½ TSP. CAYENNE PEPPER
- ¼ TSP. WHITE PEPPER
- 12 CUPS WATER
- CHOPPED RED ONION
- COOKED RICE
- SLICED JALAPEÑOS

My black beans and rice is another ez dish that complements many entrées. It is also excellent when served by itself. Soaking the beans overnight cuts down on the cooking time.

## BLACK BEANS AND RICE

(16 CUPS)

SPICY, DELICIOUS AND GOOD FOR YOU!

### PREPARATION
- ❏ Rinse beans, place in a container and cover with cold water. Refrigerate overnight.
- ❏ Heat olive oil in a large, heavy-bottomed soup pot over medium-high heat until hot.
- ❏ Add onions, green and red peppers, carrots, celery, garlic and ham hocks.
- ❏ Stir and cook for 5 minutes.
- ❏ Add parsley and all other spices and seasonings.
- ❏ Stir for 2 minutes.
- ❏ Drain and rinse the refrigerated black beans.
- ❏ Add beans to the pot and cover with 12 cups of water.
- ❏ Bring to a boil. Reduce heat and simmer for approximately 1 hour until beans are soft.
- ❏ Remove bay leaves and discard.
- ❏ Remove ham hocks, trim and shred meat.
- ❏ Place the meat back in pot, stir through beans.
- ❏ Add 2 jalapeños, seeded and minced.
- ❏ Serve beans in a bowl, garnish with chopped red onion.
- ❏ Top with cooked rice and jalapeño slices.

### RICE
Make a few cups cooked white or yellow rice according to package directions.

AS THE SUN SETS ON SARASOTA BAY, THE KLEIN FAMILY:
ED, MIMI AND ALLISON ARE ABOUT TO ENJOY
THE RARE TUNA PLATTER (PAGE 24).

These delicious, crispy potato cakes are great as an appetizer served with an omelette or alongside any entrée. Be sure to choose fresh, "rock hard" Idaho potatoes that are free from eyes. The secret to making the best latkes is to squeeze them as dry as possible before sautéing.

## POTATO PANCAKE (LATKES)

(16 LATKES)

2 EXTRA-LARGE IDAHO POTATOES (ABOUT 1 1/2 LBS.), PEELED AND IMMERSED IN ICE WATER
1 SMALL ONION
1 TBSP. ALL-PURPOSE FLOUR
1/2 TSP. SUGAR
1/4 TSP. BAKING POWDER
1/2 TSP. WHITE PEPPER
1 TSP. KOSHER SALT
1 EXTRA-LARGE EGG
CANOLA OIL FOR SAUTÉING

### PREPARATION

❑ REMOVE POTATOES FROM WATER AND PAT DRY.
❑ USING THE LARGE HOLES OF A HAND GRATER, GRATE POTATOES AND ONION.
❑ MIX POTATO AND ONION GRATINGS TOGETHER.
❑ PLACE MIXTURE IN A MESH COLANDER OR CHEESE CLOTH AND SQUEEZE TIGHTLY UNTIL MOST OF THE LIQUID IS REMOVED. THE DRYER THE POTATO, THE BETTER THE LATKE.
❑ REMOVE GRATINGS FROM COLANDER AND PLACE IN A MEDIUM-SIZE BOWL.
❑ MIX IN OTHER INGREDIENTS.
❑ HEAT 1/4 INCH OF CANOLA OIL IN A SAUTÉ PAN OVER MEDIUM-HIGH HEAT UNTIL HOT BUT NOT SMOKING.
❑ FORM LATKES INTO PATTIES, WHICHEVER SIZE YOU DESIRE. I MAKE THEM ABOUT 3 INCHES ACROSS AND NOT TOO THICK (THEY SHOULD BE QUITE THIN).
❑ SAUTÉ IN HOT OIL UNTIL BROWN AND CRISPY ON THE BOTTOM. TURN AND BROWN THE OTHER SIDE.
❑ DRAIN ON PAPER TOWEL.
❑ SERVE WITH HOMEMADE APPLESAUCE AND SOUR CREAM IF DESIRED.

HOMEMADE APPLESAUCE SEE PAGE 94

71

GARLIC, FRESH HERBS, AND DIJON
MUSTARD REALLY GO WELL WITH LAMB.
THE MUSTARD'S SHARPNESS HIGHLIGHTS
THE MILD TASTE OF A GOOD LAMB RACK.

PREHEAT OVEN TO 400°

| | |
|---|---|
| 1 | RACK OF LAMB, APPROXIMATELY 1 LB. (TRIMMED) |
| 4 | HEAPING TBSP. DIJON MUSTARD |
| 1 | TBSP. WHITE WINE |
| 2 | LARGE GARLIC CLOVES, MINCED OR CRUSHED |
| 1 | TSP. FRESH ROSEMARY, MINCED |
| 1 | TSP. FRESH BASIL, MINCED |
| 1 | TSP. FRESH TARRAGON, MINCED |
| 1 | TSP. FRESH PARSLEY, MINCED |

KOSHER SALT
BLACK PEPPER

## PREPARATION

❑ SEASON LAMB RACK WITH KOSHER SALT
AND BLACK PEPPER.

❑ IF GRILLING LAMB, SIMPLY PLACE ON
A HOT GRILL AFTER SEASONING AND
SEAR UNTIL BROWN ON ALL SIDES.

❑ IF COOKING ON A RANGE, HEAT A LITTLE
OLIVE OIL IN A LARGE SKILLET UNTIL OIL
IS VERY HOT BUT NOT SMOKING.

❑ SEAR ON ALL SIDES UNTIL NICELY
BROWNED.

❑ REMOVE FROM HEAT AND SET ASIDE.

❑ MIX ALL OF THE OTHER INGREDIENTS
TOGETHER IN BOWL, MAKING SURE THEY
ARE WELL BLENDED.

❑ SPREAD ENTIRE MIXTURE OVER MEATY
SIDE OF RACK.

❑ PLACE LAMB IN A BAKING PAN AND
COOK IN PREHEATED OVEN FOR 10
MINUTES FOR MEDIUM RARE.

❑ LET SIT FOR 5 MINUTES BEFORE SLICING
INTO DOUBLE CHOPS AND SERVE.

LAMB
WITH
GARLIC
MUSTARD
AND
FRESH HERBS

(SERVES 1 - 2)

73

# GRILLED QUAIL WITH VEGETABLES

(1 QUAIL PER SERVING)

I KEEP THIS DISH EXTREMELY SIMPLE AS THE RICH, NATURAL FLAVOR OF THE QUAIL SPEAKS FOR ITSELF. A LITTLE SEASONING, SOME SALT, PEPPER AND FRESH HERBS ARE ALL YOU NEED. THE QUAIL IS ESPECIALLY TASTY WHEN SERVED WITH GRILLED VEGETABLES, SALAD, AND GARLIC BREAD.

PREHEAT GRILL TO HIGH

1  QUAIL PER SERVING
1  SPRIG OF FRESH THYME
1  SPRIG OF FRESH ROSEMARY
KOSHER SALT & BLACK PEPPER
OLIVE OIL FOR BRUSHING

## PREPARATION

- ❑ WASH QUAIL THOROUGHLY.
- ❑ BRUSH THE QUAIL WITH OLIVE OIL.
- ❑ SEASON INSIDE AND OUT WITH KOSHER SALT AND PEPPER.
- ❑ TUCK HERBS INSIDE QUAIL.
- ❑ LOWER GRILL TO MEDIUM HEAT.
- ❑ PLACE QUAIL ON GRILL AND COOK FOR 4 MINUTES ON EACH SIDE.
- ❑ RETURN TO HIGH HEAT AND CRISP SKIN FOR 1 MINUTE, EACH SIDE.
- ❑ SERVE WITH GRILLED VEGETABLES.

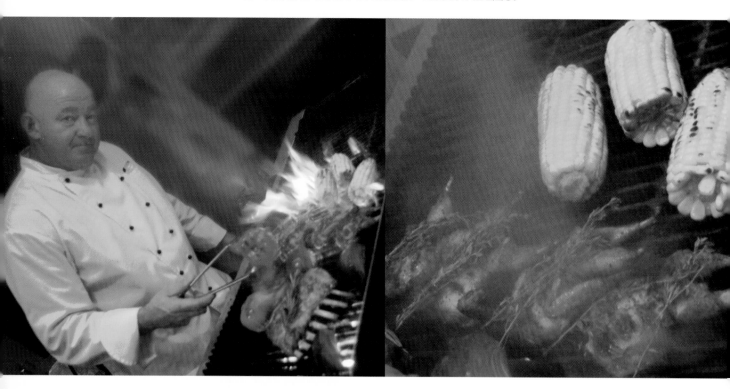

## GRILLED VEGETABLES

WHEN I NEED THE BEST VEGETABLES AVAILABLE, I GO TO GERALDSON`S BARN IN BRADENTON (FL). I AM NEVER DISAPPOINTED. IN THE FIELD BEHIND THE RUSTIC BARN GROWS ROUND ZUCCHINI, MULTI-COLORED BABY EGGPLANT, TREASURE CAVE CORN, AND THE BEST TOMATOES IN FLORIDA!

PREHEAT GRILL TO MEDIUM

| | |
|---|---|
| 1 | CUP OLIVE OIL |
| 6 | CLOVES OF GARLIC, MINCED |
| 1/2 | CUP BASIL, CHOPPED |

KOSHER SALT
BLACK PEPPER
RED ONIONS, QUARTERED
BABY COLORED EGGPLANTS
GREEN, RED, YELLOW PEPPERS
BABY ZUCCHINI
YELLOW SQUASH
\* EGGPLANTS, PEPPERS, ZUCCHINI, AND
 SQUASH ALL SLICED IN HALF
WHOLE MUSHROOMS

## PREPARATION
❑ HEAT OLIVE OIL IN A MEDIUM SAUCE PAN UNTIL HOT BUT NOT SMOKING.
❑ REMOVE FROM HEAT AND STIR IN GARLIC AND BASIL.
❑ BRUSH VEGETABLES WITH GARLIC/BASIL OIL AND SEASON WITH SALT AND PEPPER.
❑ REDUCE HEAT TO MEDIUM.
❑ PLACE ON GRILL AND COOK VEGETABLES UNTIL DONE.

## Smoked BBQ Baby Back Ribs

(SERVES 4)

| 4 | RACKS, PORK BABY BACK RIBS |
|---|---|
| 1 | TBSP. KOSHER SALT |
| 2 | TBSP. WHOLE BLACK PEPPER |
| 2 | TBSP. PICKLING SPICE |
| 1/4 | TSP. CAYENNE PEPPER |
| 1/2 | CUP RED WINE VINEGAR |

A FEW HANDFULS OF WOOD CHIPS (HICKORY OR MESQUITE), SOAKED IN WATER FOR AT LEAST 15 MINUTES.

### PREPARATION

❑ PLACE RIBS IN A LARGE POT AND COVER WITH WATER.
❑ SET ASIDE WOOD CHIPS.
❑ ADD ALL INGREDIENTS TO POT AND BRING TO A BOIL, THEN REDUCE HEAT. LET SIMMER FOR 30 MINUTES.
❑ REMOVE RIBS FROM HEAT, RINSE WITH COLD WATER.
❑ REMOVE FAT FROM UNDERSIDE OF COOLED RIBS.
❑ FIRE UP GRILL TO HIGH HEAT AS YOU PREPARE BBQ SAUCE.

### BBQ SAUCE

| 6 | LARGE GARLIC CLOVES, MINCED |
|---|---|
| 1 | 32 OZ. BOTTLE OF KETCHUP |
| 3 | TBSP. DIJON MUSTARD |
| 3/4 | CUP RED WINE VINEGAR |
| 1 | CUP (PACKED) BROWN SUGAR |
| 1 | TBSP. DRY MUSTARD |
| 1 | TSP. RED PEPPER FLAKES |
| 1/4 | TSP. CAYENNE PEPPER |

JUICE OF 2 LEMONS
OLIVE OIL FOR SAUTÉING

### PREPARATION

❑ SAUTÈ GARLIC IN OLIVE OIL, COOK UNTIL GARLIC IS LIGHTLY BROWN.
❑ ADD REMAINING INGREDIENTS AND BRING TO A BOIL.
❑ REDUCE TO SIMMER, COOK FOR 20 MINUTES.
❑ REMOVE SAUCE FROM HEAT. REDUCE GRILL HEAT TO MEDIUM.
❑ PLACE SOAKED WOOD CHIPS ON THE FLAME IN THE GRILL.
❑ COAT BOTH SIDES OF RIBS WITH BBQ SAUCE.
❑ PLACE RIBS ON GRILL AND COOK EACH SIDE UNTIL RIBS BEGIN TO BLISTER.
❑ SERVE WITH EXTRA SAUCE ON THE SIDE.

76

FRANK BROWN IS WHAT WE CALL IN THE BUSINESS A "SALT AND PEPPER COOK." HE USES VERY LITTLE SEASONINGS OTHER THAN SALT AND PEPPER. I DON'T KNOW IF HE'S THE BEST SOUTHERN-STYLE COOK I'VE EVER MET, BUT WHEN THEY GIVE A ROLL CALL FOR THAT DISTINCTION, THERE WON'T BE MANY AHEAD OF HIM IN LINE. HERE'S TWO OF HIS SIGNATURE RECIPES. WAIT UNTIL YOU TRY THESE!

## FRANK BROWN'S GREEN BEANS, POTATOES, AND BACON

(SERVES 4)

| | |
|---|---|
| 1 | LB. FRESH GREEN BEANS, STEMMED |
| 2 | TSP. SALT |
| 1/2 | TSP. BAKING SODA |
| 1 | EXTRA-LARGE IDAHO POTATO, PEELED AND CUT INTO 2 INCH CUBES |
| 3 | STRIPS BACON, CUT INTO SMALL PIECES |
| 1 | SMALL ONION, MINCED |

SALT AND PEPPER

FRANK BROWN, ALWAYS FULL OF SURPRISES.

### PREPARATION

❑ PLACE GREEN BEANS IN A SAUCEPAN, COVER WITH WATER. ADD 1 TSP. SALT AND BAKING SODA.
❑ BRING TO A BOIL. REDUCE HEAT TO SIMMER.
❑ COOK STRING BEANS FOR 5 MINUTES. DRAIN, RINSE WITH COLD WATER, SET ASIDE.

❑ PLACE POTATO CUBES IN A SAUCEPAN, COVER WITH WATER. ADD 1 TSP. SALT, BRING TO A BOIL.
❑ COOK UNTIL JUST DONE (DON'T OVERCOOK).
❑ DRAIN AND SET ASIDE.
❑ SAUTÉ BACON PIECES OVER MEDIUM-HIGH HEAT UNTIL CRISP.
❑ ADD ONION AND COOK FOR 2 MINUTES.
❑ ADD GREEN BEANS AND POTATOES.
❑ COOK FOR ANOTHER 3 MINUTES WHILE STIRRING CONSTANTLY (POTATOES WILL BREAK UP A LITTLE, COATING GREEN BEANS).
❑ SALT AND PEPPER TO TASTE.

## STEWED OKRA, TOMATOES & RED ONIONS

(4 servings)

2     LARGE GARLIC CLOVES, MINCED
$\frac{1}{2}$     CUP RED ONION, CHOPPED
1     LB. OKRA, CUT INTO 1 INCH PIECES
1     LARGE RIPE TOMATO, CHOPPED
4     SPRIGS FRESH THYME
OLIVE OIL FOR SAUTÉING
SALT AND PEPPER TO TASTE

### PREPARATION

- ❏ HEAT OIL IN SAUTÉ PAN OVER MEDIUM HEAT UNTIL HOT.
- ❏ ADD GARLIC AND ONIONS, SAUTÉ FOR 3 MINUTES.
- ❏ ADD OKRA, THYME, AND COOK FOR ANOTHER 3 MINUTES, STIRRING FREQUENTLY.
- ❏ BLEND IN TOMATOES, ADD SALT AND PEPPER.
- ❏ LOWER THE HEAT.
- ❏ COVER THE PAN WITH A LID, LET SIMMER FOR 5 MINUTES.
- ❏ SERVE IMMEDIATELY. SEASON WITH SALT AND PEPPER.

# Roesti Potatoes
## (Swiss-Style Hash Browns)

(1 potato serves 2)

Roesti potatoes are perfect for mopping up a sauce. Consider rich gravy dishes such as shredded swiss veal, beef goulash, and chicken fricassee. Dishes like these were made for potatoes that absorb their sauces like a sponge.

Use whole, extra-large idaho potatoes. The amount you need will depend on how many servings you prepare.

## PREPARATION
- ❏ Cook potatoes (with skins on) a day ahead of time.
- ❏ Boil them in salted water until a fork barely penetrates centers, about 12 minutes (you want them a little underdone).
- ❏ Drain, then refrigerate until the next day.
- ❏ Peel cold potatoes and then coarsely hand grate them.
- ❏ Salt and pepper the potatoes.
- ❏ Heat ¼-inch canola oil in a sauté pan until very hot.
- ❏ Add potatoes.
- ❏ Fry until very crisp. Garnish with some crisp bacon or onions.
- ❏ Drain on paper towels and serve.

PREHEAT OVEN TO 350°

| | |
|---|---|
| 3 | LB. PIECE OF CENTER-CUT PORK LOIN |
| 1 ½ | CUP OLIVE OIL |
| 2 | SPRIGS EACH OF FRESH ROSEMARY, BASIL, THYME AND OREGANO (STEMMED, LEAVES ONLY) |
| 6 | LARGE GARLIC CLOVES |
| 2 | CUPS WHITE WINE (CHARDONNAY OR CHABLIS) |
| 2 | CUPS WATER |
| 4 | LARGE CARROTS, PEELED AND CUT INTO 3 INCH PIECES |
| 2 | LARGE ONIONS, PEELED AND QUARTERED |

KOSHER SALT AND GROUND BLACK PEPPER

Crusted Roast
Pork Loin

Here's a good recipe which involves a little preparation in the beginning. While the pork is roasting in the oven, you can prepare the rest of the meal. The garlic and herb crust that encases the tender meat really sets it off.

# CRUSTED ROAST PORK LOIN

(SERVES 6)

## PREPARATION

- ❑ Season pork loin with salt & pepper.
- ❑ Pour olive oil into food processor or blender.
- ❑ Add fresh herbs, garlic, and blend to a paste.
- ❑ Rub paste over pork loin, coating entire piece of meat.
- ❑ Heat a heavy skillet over medium-high heat (make sure it is hot enough for searing).
- ❑ Carefully place "pasted" pork loin into the skillet, searing it on all sides until it is evenly browned.
- ❑ Place carrots, onions and celery close together in the bottom of a roasting pan.
- ❑ Remove pork loin from skillet, place atop vegetables in pan.
- ❑ Pour the 2 cups of wine into hot skillet and stir for 3 minutes.
- ❑ Slowly pour wine and 2 cups of water into the pan (not directly on the pork).
- ❑ Roast about 2 hours or until your meat thermometer registers 165°.
- ❑ Remove pork from oven and cover loosely with a piece of foil. Let sit for 20 minutes before carving.
- ❑ Slice and serve with carrots, onions, and celery.
- ❑ Mashed yukon gold potatoes go well with this dish.

# CORN FRITTERS

## (24 FRITTERS)

JACK FASSETT AND CHARLIE WALTERS ARE TWO OF THE GREATEST COOKS I HAVE EVER WORKED WITH. JACK AND CHARLIE WERE IN THE BUSINESS FOR OVER 50 YEARS. JACK WAS A BAKER AND CHARLIE A "SCRATCH COOK." IT WASN'T EASY TO GET THEIR RECIPES, SO I HAD TO BE DEVIOUS. DURING SUNDAY BRUNCH AT THE LONGBOAT KEY CLUB, I WOULD SAY TO EITHER CHARLIE OR JACK THAT THE OTHER COOK'S BATTER FOR CORN FRITTERS WAS BETTER. IN THE END, EACH ONE OFFERED ME HIS RECIPE AND THEY WERE EXACTLY THE SAME! SO, HERE IS THE BEST CORN FRITTER RECIPE YOU'LL EVER NEED. THE BATTER IS ACTUALLY BETTER IF MADE A DAY AHEAD OF TIME AND REFRIGERATED.

| | |
|---|---|
| 2 | CUPS ALL-PURPOSE FLOUR |
| 4 | TSP. BAKING POWDER |
| 1/4 | CUP SUGAR |
| 1 | TSP. SALT |
| 2 | EGGS |
| 1 | 15 OZ. CAN OF CREAMED CORN (YELLOW OR WHITE) |

OIL FOR FRYING
CINNAMON SUGAR AND MAPLE SYRUP

## PREPARATION

- ❏ MIX TOGETHER DRY INGREDIENTS.
- ❏ ADD 2 EGGS AND CREAMED CORN.
- ❏ STIR WITH WITH A WOODEN SPOON UNTIL WELL BLENDED.
- ❏ HEAT ABOUT 2 INCHES OF CANOLA OIL IN HEAVY, WALLED POT (ABOUT 375°).
- ❏ DIP A TABLESPOON INTO THE HOT OIL (THIS WILL PREVENT THE BATTER FROM STICKING TO THE SPOON).
- ❏ SCOOP THE BATTER ONTO THE TABLESPOON AND DROP INTO THE THE OIL.
- ❏ CONTINUE THIS STEP UNTIL THE POT HAS A GOOD AMOUNT OF FRITTERS, YET IS NOT OVERCROWDED.
- ❏ WHEN THE FRITTERS FLOAT TO THE TOP OF THE OIL, TURN THEM OVER SO THAT THE OTHER SIDE COOKS.
- ❏ REMOVE FRITTERS FROM THE POT AND DRAIN ON A PAPER TOWEL.
- ❏ ROLL THE FRITTERS IN CINNAMON SUGAR AND SERVE WITH MAPLE SYRUP.

Trond and Peter's favorite food. They love them, so I have included this large recipe for the 2 Vikings.

## SCANDINAVIAN PANCAKES

LARGE RECIPE

| | |
|---|---|
| 1 | CUP SUGAR |
| 2 | CUPS ALL-PURPOSE FLOUR |
| 1 | CUP WATER |
| 1 | CUP OLIVE OIL — YEP!  THAT'S RIGHT, OLIVE OIL! |
| 18 | EXTRA-LARGE EGGS |
| 1 | TBSP. ORANGE EXTRACT |
| 1 | TBSP. LEMON EXTRACT |
| 1 | TBSP. VANILLA EXTRACT |

### PREPARATION

❑ MIX SUGAR AND FLOUR TOGETHER.

❑ ADD WATER, OLIVE OIL, 4 EGGS AND ALL EXTRACTS.

❑ STIR TOGETHER WITH A WOODEN SPOON.

❑ ADD REMAINING 14 EGGS AND CONTINUE STIRRING UNTIL SMOOTH.

❑ HEAT A NON-STICK SAUTÉ PAN OVER MEDIUM-HIGH HEAT, COAT WITH A LITTLE CANOLA OIL.

❑ SPOON MIXTURE INTO PAN AND DESIGN THE PANCAKE AS YOU WISH: SMALL, MEDIUM, OR LARGE.

❑ COOK THROUGH UNTIL GOLDEN BROWN, THEN FLIP TO COOK THE OTHER SIDE.

❑ SPRINKLE WITH POWDERED SUGAR (IF DESIRED) AND SERVE WITH YOUR FAVORITE SYRUP.

❑ FRESH FRUIT SUCH AS BANANAS, APPLES, PEACHES OR PEARS CAN BE ADDED TO YOUR PANCAKES: FIRST, SAUTÉ FRUIT IN A LITTLE BUTTER AND COVER WITH PANCAKE MIXTURE.  COOK UNTIL DONE ON BOTH SIDES, TURNING PANCAKE ONLY ONCE.

❑ TOP WITH EXTRA FRUIT IF DESIRED.

## SMALL RECIPE

| | |
|---|---|
| 1/4 | CUP SUGAR |
| 1/2 | CUP ALL-PURPOSE FLOUR |
| 1/4 | CUP WATER |
| 1/4 | CUP OLIVE OIL |
| 4 | EXTRA-LARGE EGGS |
| 1/4 | TSP. ORANGE EXTRACT |
| 1/4 | TSP. LEMON EXTRACT |
| 1/4 | TSP. VANILLA EXTRACT |

## PREPARATION

- ❏ MIX SUGAR AND FLOUR TOGETHER.
- ❏ ADD WATER, OLIVE OIL, 1 OF THE EGGS AND EXTRACTS.
- ❏ STIR TOGETHER WITH A WOODEN SPOON.
- ❏ ADD THE REMAINING 4 EGGS AND CONTINUE STIRRING UNTIL SMOOTH.
- ❏ TO COMPLETE THE RECIPE, FOLLOW THE COOKING DIRECTIONS FOR LARGER PANCAKES. TOP WITH EXTRA FRUIT IF DESIRED.

HERE IS AN EASY, ELEGANT DESSERT THAT YOU CAN MAKE AHEAD OF TIME, A BAKED MERINGUE SHELL FILLED WITH CHOCOLATE MOUSSE.  I ALWAYS MAKE BIRDS NESTS FOR MY SON ZACH'S CLASSROOM AT CHRISTMAS.  THE KIDS LOVE THEM.  THE MOUSSE IS GREAT BY ITSELF AND OTHER FILLINGS CAN BE USED IN THE MERINGUE SHELL.  ADJUST SERVINGS TO ANY SIZE YOU CHOOSE.  MINIATURE SHELLS ARE NICE, BUT THE KIDS LIKE THEM AS BIG AS THEY CAN GET THEM!

PREHEAT OVEN TO 275°

## BIRDS NESTS

DELICATE MERINGUE SHELLS FILLED WITH CREAMY CHOCOLATE MOUSSE.

8 LARGE PORTIONS OR 16 SMALL

MERINGUE SHELLS

| | |
|---|---|
| 4 | LARGE EGG WHITES |
| 1/8 | TSP. CREAM OF TARTAR |
| 1 | CUP OF SUGAR |
| 3/4 | TSP. VANILLA EXTRACT |

## PREPARATION

❏ USING A MIXER, BEAT EGG WHITES UNTIL SOFT PEAKS FORM, THEN ADD VANILLA.
❏ SLOWLY ADD SUGAR IN SMALL AMOUNTS.
❏ BEAT UNTIL SUGAR IS DISSOLVED AND EGG WHITES BECOME GLOSSY AND STIFF.
❏ LINE A COOKIE SHEET WITH ALUMINUM FOIL.
❏ PLACE MERINGUE INTO A PASTRY BAG AND PIPE SWIRLS OF APPROX. 5 INCHES IN DIAMETER ONTO COOKIE SHEET (YOU CAN DECIDE HOW MANY SWIRLS HIGH YOU WISH TO MAKE).
❏ IF YOU ARE NOT USING A PASTRY BAG, YOU CAN SPOON DOLLOPS OF MERINGUE ONTO COOKIE SHEET AND SCOOP OUT CENTER TO CREATE A HOLLOW FOR YOUR FILLING.
❏ BAKE MERINGUE AT 275° FOR 1 HOUR, THEN TURN THE OVEN OFF.
❏ LEAVE MERINGUE IN OVEN FOR AN ADDITIONAL HOUR OR UNTIL DRY.
❏ TAKE FROM OVEN AND LET STAND FOR ANOTHER 20 MINUTES.
❏ REMOVE MERINGUE FROM COOKIE SHEET WHEN IT HAS COOLED.

(CONTINUES ON NEXT PAGE )

## BIRDS NESTS

(CONTINUED)

### CHOCOLATE MOUSSE

| | |
|---|---|
| 1/4 | CUP SUGAR |
| 4 | TBSP. LIQUOR (YOUR CHOICE: BRANDY, AMARETTO, DARK RUM, KAHLÚA, ETC.) |
| 4 | OZ. SEMISWEET CHOCOLATE (PIECES OR MORSELS) |
| 1/4 | CUP BREWED COFFEE |
| 2 | EGG WHITES |
| 2 | CUPS HEAVY CREAM |
| 1/4 | TSP. VANILLA EXTRACT |

### PREPARATION

❑ HEAT THE LIQUOR IN A SMALL SAUCEPAN OVER LOW HEAT *(DO NOT OVERHEAT LIQUOR).

❑ STIR IN SUGAR AND COOK UNTIL SUGAR MELTS AND MIXTURE BECOMES SYRUPY. DO NOT BURN MIXTURE.

❑ PLACE CHOCOLATE PIECES AND COFFEE IN A MICROWAVE-SAFE BOWL.

❑ MICROWAVE FOR 30 SECONDS, THEN STIR WITH A WOODEN SPOON. REPEAT PROCEDURE 3 TIMES, STIRRING UNTIL MIXTURE IS SMOOTH.

❑ A SMALL AMOUNT OF WARM WATER CAN BE ADDED IF MIXTURE BECOMES TOO THICK.

❑ ADD SYRUP TO THE CHOCOLATE AND STIR WITH WOODEN SPOON UNTIL WELL BLENDED. SET ASIDE.

❑ USING A HANDHELD OR STATIONARY MIXER, BEAT THE EGG WHITES UNTIL STIFF AND GLOSSY. SOFT PEAKS WILL BEGIN TO FORM. SET ASIDE

❑ USING A HANDHELD OR STATIONARY MIXER, WHIP HEAVY CREAM AND VANILLA UNTIL FULL-BODIED AND THICK.

❑ USING A RUBBER SPATULA, GENTLY FOLD EGG WHITES INTO THE HEAVY CREAM AND VANILLA MIXTURE.

❑ NEXT, FOLD CHOCOLATE INTO THE MIXTURE OF EGG WHITES, HEAVY CREAM AND VANILLA.

❑ CHILL.

❑ SPOON MOUSSE INTO MERINGUE SHELLS, TOP WITH CHOCOLATE MORSELS AND SERVE.

. Alan Treiman,
wife Lenore and daughter Nicole
Ready for dessert.
ef Joe is holding Leo "the wonder dog."

A LIGHT, CREAMY DESSERT THAT COMPLIMENTS ANY MEAL
AND IS EASY TO PREPARE.  IT CAN BE MADE A DAY AHEAD OF
TIME IF DESIRED.  THE POACHED ORANGES FINISH IT OFF
NICELY.

PREHEAT OVEN TO 325°

| | |
|---|---|
| ¹/₂ | CUP WATER |
| 1 | CUP SUGAR |
| 4 | EXTRA-LARGE EGGS |
| 2 | CUPS WHOLE MILK |
| 1 | TSP. VANILLA EXTRACT |
| PINCH OF SALT | |

# CRÈME CARAMEL WITH POACHED ORANGES
(SERVES 6)

ELITHA & DANIEL KANE
DISCUSS SOME LAST
MINUTE PARTY DETAILS.

## PREPARATION

❑ MIX WATER AND ¹/₂ CUP SUGAR IN
   A SMALL SAUCE PAN.
❑ COOK OVER MEDIUM HEAT UNTIL
   MIXTURE TURNS INTO A CARAMEL
   COLORED SYRUP (ABOUT 5 MINUTES).
❑ POUR SYRUP EQUALLY INTO 6 RAMEKINS.
   LET STAND FOR A FEW MINUTES.
❑ WHISK REMAINING SUGAR AND EGGS
   TOGETHER IN A BOWL.
❑ ADD MILK, VANILLA AND SALT, STIRRING
   UNTIL WELL BLENDED.
❑ POUR INTO RAMEKINS.
❑ PLACE RAMEKINS IN A BAKING PAN.
❑ FILL BAKING PAN WITH HOT WATER HALF
   WAY UP THE SIDES OF THE RAMEKINS
   (THIS IS CALLED A WATERBATH).
❑ PLACE IN OVEN AND COOK FOR 50 TO
   60 MINUTES UNTIL THE MIXTURE SETS.
❑ REMOVE RAMEKINS FROM PAN
   AND LET COOL.
❑ COVER AND REFRIGERATE.
   WHEN SERVING:  RUN A SHARP KNIFE
   AROUND INSIDE EDGE OF RAMEKIN TO
   DISLODGE THE CUSTARD AND TURN IT
   UPSIDE DOWN ON YOUR SERVING PLATE.
❑ GARNISH WITH POACHED ORANGES.

93

| 4 | SEEDLESS ORANGES |
| 1/2 | CUP HONEY |
| 2 | CUPS WHITE WINE (CHARDONNAY OR CHABLIS) |

## POACHED ORANGES

### PREPARATION

- ❏ PEEL ORANGES, LEAVING WHITE MEMBRANE INTACT.
- ❏ SLICE PEELED SKIN VERY FINELY, CREATING A ZEST.
- ❏ PLACE SUGAR, HONEY AND WATER IN A SMALL SAUCE PAN AT MEDIUM-HIGH HEAT AND BRING TO A BOIL.
- ❏ BOIL FOR 3 MINUTES.
- ❏ CUT AWAY WHITE ORANGE MEMBRANE AND PLACE ORANGES INTO SAUCEPAN.
- ❏ CONTINUE TO COOK FOR 3 MINUTES, STIRRING GENTLY.
- ❏ REMOVE ORANGES AND PLACE IN BOWL, LEAVING SYRUP IN SAUCE PAN.
- ❏ ADD THE ZEST TO SYRUP AND COOK FOR AN ADDITIONAL 2 MINUTES.
- ❏ POUR ZEST AND SYRUP OVER ORANGES AND CHILL UNTIL SERVING TIME.
- ❏ SERVE CRÈME CARAMEL SPRINKLED WITH ORANGE ZEST AND POACHED ORANGES.

## CHEF JOE'S HOMEMADE APPLESAUCE

TAKE SEVERAL OF YOUR FAVORITE BRANDS OF APPLES, WASH AND CORE THEM WELL. LEAVE THE SKIN ON. CUT INTO CHUNKS AND BLEND THEM WITH A LITTLE CINNAMON, OR NUTMEG IN A FOOD PROCESSOR.

FAST, EZ AND DELICIOUS.

THIS DESSERT IS A CHALLENGE AND MAY TAKE A FEW TRIES TO PERFECT, BUT IT IS WELL WORTH THE EFFORT. ONCE YOU GET THE METHOD DOWN, YOU'LL BE MAKING THEM ALL THE TIME. THEY COMPLIMENT ANY MEAL PERFECTLY. I HAVE ADDED A RECIPE FOR A CHOCOLATE SAUCE THAT SENDS THESE DESSERTS OVER THE TOP.

# CREAM PUFFS WITH CHOCOLATE SAUCE
## (2 DOZEN)

PREHEAT OVEN TO 450°

| | |
|---|---|
| 1 | CUP WATER |
| 1/2 | STICK BUTTER |
| 1 1/4 | CUPS SIFTED, ALL-PURPOSE FLOUR |
| 1/4 | TSP. SALT |
| 5 | EXTRA-LARGE EGGS |
| 1 | EXTRA-LARGE EGG WHITE |

CUSTARD FILLING
POWDERED SUGAR

## PREPARATION

❑ COOK BUTTER AND WATER IN A HEAVY SAUCE PAN OVER MEDIUM-HIGH HEAT UNTIL BUTTER IS MELTED AND LIQUID COMES TO A BOIL.

❑ ADD FLOUR AND SALT WHILE STIRRING VIGOROUSLY WITH A WOODEN SPOON.

❑ STIR UNTIL MIXTURE PULLS FROM SIDE OF THE SAUCE PAN.

❑ TURN OFF HEAT.

❑ ADD EGGS TO MIXTURE ONE AT A TIME, BEATING WELL WITH WOODEN SPOON.

❑ BLEND EACH EGG INTO MIXTURE THOROUGHLY BEFORE ADDING ANOTHER.

❑ BEAT UNTIL SMOOTH AND SET ASIDE TO COOL.

❑ POUR COOLED MIXTURE INTO A PASTRY BAG WITH A PLAIN TIP.

❑ PIPE MIXTURE ONTO A LIGHTLY GREASED SHEET PAN IN SMALL MOUNDS (CREAM PUFF SIZE) AND SPACE 2 INCHES APART.

❑ BAKE ON MIDDLE RACK FOR 8 MINUTES.

(CONTINUES ON NEXT PAGE )

❏ Reduce heat to 350° and bake for an additional 30 minutes. Remove from heat and let cool on a wire rack.
❏ Fill with custard (custard recipe follows).

## CREAM PUFFS WITH CHOCOLATE SAUCE

(CONTINUED)

CUSTARD FILLING

| 4 | CUPS WHOLE MILK |
| 1 | CUP SUGAR |
| 1 | TSP. VANILLA |
| 4 | EXTRA-LARGE EGG YOLKS |
| 3/4 | CUPS CORN STARCH |

### PREPARATION

❏ Heat 3 cups of milk, sugar and vanilla in a heavy-bottomed sauce pan.
❏ Bring to a high simmer, stirring constantly.
❏ Mix 1 cup milk with 4 egg yolks and corn starch in a bowl, stir until well blended and smooth. Add to simmering milk. Stir until custard thickens.
❏ Lower heat and cook for several minutes (stirring).
❏ Remove from heat, cool, and place in pastry bag.
❏ Use a small knife to make a tiny hole in the side of each puff. Pipe custard into each puff.
❏ Dust generously with confectioner's sugar.

CHOCOLATE SAUCE

| 8 | OZ. SEMISWEET CHOCOLATE PIECES |
| 2 | TBSP. UNSALTED BUTTER |
| 1/2 | CUP HEAVY CREAM |

### PREPARATION

❏ Melt chocolate and butter in microwave for 1 minute and 30 seconds. Stir vigorously, until smooth.
❏ Heat heavy cream in sauce pan until simmering. Stir in chocolate mixture and bring to a boil.
❏ Remove from heat and cool.
❏ Coat cream puffs with chocolate sauce and serve.

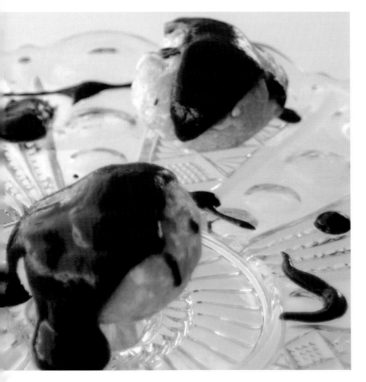

A RICH AND CREAMY, SMOOTH-AS-SILK DESSERT WITH A THIN
CRUST OF BROWNED SUGAR ON TOP.  SIMPLE TO MAKE AND
EASY TO SERVE.

## WHITE CHOCOLATE CRÈME BRULÉE

(SERVES 6)

PREHEAT OVEN TO 325°

| 2 | CUPS HEAVY CREAM |
| 4 | OZ. WHITE CHOCOLATE BROKEN INTO PIECES |
| 5 | EXTRA-LARGE EGG YOLKS |
| 1/4 | CUP SUGAR |
| 1 | TSP. VANILLA EXTRACT |

BROWN SUGAR FOR CRUSTING THE TOP

### PREPARATION

- ❑ HEAT HEAVY CREAM IN THICK-WALLED POT OVER MEDIUM HEAT UNTIL IT STARTS TO SIMMER.
- ❑ TURN OFF HEAT.
- ❑ ADD WHITE CHOCOLATE, SUGAR, VANILLA.
- ❑ STIR UNTIL CHOCOLATE HAS MELTED.
- ❑ WHISK IN EGG YOLKS.
- ❑ POUR CREAM MIXTURE INTO 6 RAMEKINS AND PLACE IN A BAKING PAN.
- ❑ FILL BAKING PAN WITH HOT WATER HALF WAY UP THE SIDES OF THE RAMEKINS.

- ❑ PUT IN OVEN AND BAKE FOR 45 MINUTES.
- ❑ REMOVE RAMEKINS FROM BAKING PAN, DRAIN WATER.  RETURN RAMEKINS TO THE BAKING PAN AND PLACE SOME ICE CUBES AROUND THEM.
- ❑ TURN OVEN TEMPERATURE TO BROIL.
- ❑ PLACE BROWN SUGAR INTO A FINE MESH SIEVE OR STRAINER.
- ❑ SHAKE SUGAR OVER BRULÉE, FORMING A FINE COATING ON TOP.
- ❑ RETURN BAKING PAN TO OVEN AND PLACE ON TOP RACK.
- ❑ LET BRULÉE BROWN UNDER BROILER UNTIL SUGAR BUBBLES.
- ❑ THIS TAKES ONLY A FEW MINUTES (IF LEFT UNDER THE BROILER TOO LONG SUGAR WILL BURN).
- ❑ REMOVE FROM OVEN AND COOL DOWN.
- ❑ COVER AND REFRIGERATE UNTIL SERVING.

"ANOTHER PERFECT DAY IN PARADISE"
KEMP AND BEVERLY RIECHMANN
RELAX WITH A GLASS OF FINE MERLOT"

FLORIDA'S ALL TIME FAVORITE DESSERT. THIS LIGHT, REFRESHING ZESTY TREAT IS ALWAYS A WINNER, THE PERFECT END TO ANY MEAL.

PREHEAT OVEN TO 350° DEGREES

# KEY LIME PIE

(SERVES 8)

## KEY LIME PIE CRUST
| | |
|---|---|
| 4 | CUPS GRAHAM CRACKER CRUMBS |
| 8 | OZ MELTED UNSALTED BUTTER (2 STICKS) |
| 1/4 | CUP GRANULATED SUGAR |
| 1 | TSP. CINNAMON |

## PREPARATION
- ❏ MIX ALL INGREDIENTS TOGETHER UNTIL COMBINED.
- ❏ PRESS GRAHAM CRACKER CRUMB MIXTURE INTO THE BOTTOM OF A 9 INCH GLASS PIE PLATE AND UP THE SIDE, AT LEAST 1/4 INCH THICK.
- ❏ PLACE PIE SHELL INTO OVEN AND BAKE FOR 10 MINUTES.
- ❏ REMOVE AND LET COOL.

## KEY LIME PIE
| | |
|---|---|
| 8 | EXTRA LARGE-EGG YOLKS |
| 2 | CANS (14 OZ. EACH) SWEETENED CONDENSED MILK |
| 1 | CUP FRESH SQUEEZED KEY LIME JUICE |

## PREPARATION
- ❏ BEAT 8 EGG YOLKS WITH AN ELECTRIC MIXER ON HIGH SPEED FOR 8 MINUTES; THEY WILL BE THICK AND CREAMY.
- ❏ TURN OFF MIXER AND ADD THE 2 CANS OF SWEETENED CONDENSED MILK, BEAT FOR 30 SECONDS ON MEDIUM SPEED, TURN OFF MIXER, SCRAPE DOWN BOWL AND THEN BEAT FOR ANOTHER 30 SECONDS.
- ❏ WITH MIXER STILL RUNNING ON MEDIUM SPEED ADD THE 1 CUP OF KEY LIME JUICE AND BEAT FOR 30 SECONDS, TURN OFF MIXER, SCRAPE DOWN BOWL AND THEN BEAT FOR ANOTHER 30 SECONDS.
- ❏ PLACE MIXTURE INTO THE PIE SHELL AND PLACE IN THE OVEN FOR 15 MINUTES, REMOVE AND LET COOL.
- ❏ REFRIGERATE PIE UNTIL CHILLED. TOP WITH FRESH WHIPPED CREAM AND LIME ZEST.

This elegant dessert is fairly simple to make. However, it requires ample preparation time. The bulk of the work can be done the day before, with the exception of the browning of the meringue and the flaming of the 'Alaska' at the table. Believe me, your guests will definitely be impressed. Baked alaska is chocolate cake that is sliced in half, splashed with brandy or kirsch, filled with ice cream, covered with meringue, then browned in a hot oven and finally flamed at the table to the delight of your guests. You can do this! Like everything else, just take your time.

# Baked Alaska

## (serves 8)

PREHEAT OVEN TO 350°

### CHOCOLATE CAKE

| | |
|---|---|
| 1 | CUP BOILING WATER |
| 3/4 | CUP BAKING COCOA |
| 2 | CUPS ALL-PURPOSE FLOUR |
| 1 | TSP. BAKING SODA |
| 1 | TSP. BAKING POWDER |
| 1/2 | TSP. SALT |
| 1 3/4 | CUPS SUGAR |
| 1 1/2 | STICKS (6 OZ.) BUTTER, SOFTENED |
| 1 | TSP. VANILLA EXTRACT |
| 2 | EXTRA-LARGE EGGS |

BRANDY OR KIRSCH

## PREPARATION

❑ Dissolve cocoa in boiling water and set aside.
❑ Beat sugar, butter and vanilla together with a mixer until thick and creamy (about 5 minutes).
❑ Add each egg one at a time, beating mixture well after each addition.
❑ Combine and mix flour, baking soda, baking powder and salt.
❑ With mixer setting on low speed, add dry ingredients to the creamed mixture.
❑ Scrape down sides of bowl and beat on medium speed for 2 minutes.

(CONTINUES ON NEXT PAGE )

## BAKED ALASKA

(CONTINUED)

- ❏ SLOWLY ADD DISSOLVED COCOA, SCRAPE DOWN THE BOWL, BEAT 1 MINUTE.
- ❏ GREASE AND LIGHTLY FLOUR A 10 INCH TUBE PAN WITH BUTTER OR MARGARINE.
- ❏ POUR BATTER INTO PAN AND BAKE AT 350° FOR 30 - 35 MINUTES.
- ❏ CHECK WITH A WOODEN TOOTHPICK IN THE CENTER FOR DONENESS.
- ❏ GENTLY TAKE CAKE FROM OVEN AND SET ASIDE FOR ABOUT 30 MINUTES.
- ❏ REMOVE FROM PAN AND REST ON A WIRE RACK UNTIL COMPLETELY COOLED.
- ❏ WRAP CAKE IN FILM WRAP AND REFRIGERATE UNTIL COLD (ABOUT 2 HOURS).

NOW THAT YOUR CAKE IS DONE, THE REST IS SIMPLE TO DO.

- ❏ REMOVE COLD CAKE FROM THE REFRIGERATOR, SLICE IN HALF.
- ❏ SPLASH CAKE HALVES LIBERALLY WITH KIRSCH OR BRANDY.
- ❏ MOUND VANILLA ICE CREAM BETWEEN CAKE HALVES.
- ❏ COVER WITH FILM WRAP AND PLACE IN FREEZER.

YOU'RE JUST ABOUT DONE.
IT'S TIME TO MAKE THE MERINGUE.

### MERINGUE

SOME TIPS FOR GOOD MERINGUE:

- ❏ USE VERY CLEAN AND DRY BEATERS, BOWLS AND STAINLESS STEEL COOKWARE (NO PLASTIC).
- ❏ ABSOLUTELY NO TRACES OF YOLK IN THE EGG WHITES.
- ❏ BEAT THE SUGAR IN GRADUALLY, 2 TABLESPOONS AT A TIME.
- ❏ DISSOLVE ALL SUGAR.

| | |
|---|---|
| 6 | EGG WHITES (SAVE HALF AN EGG SHELL FOR PRESENTATION) |
| 1 1/2 | CUPS SUGAR |
| 1/4 | TSP. CREAM OF TARTAR |
| 1 | TSP. VANILLA EXTRACT |

(CONTINUES ON PAGE 110 )

## BAKED
## ALASKA
(CONTINUED)

**PREPARATION**

❑ USING A MIXER, BEAT EGG WHITES AND CREAM OF TARTAR ON HIGH SPEED.

❑ GRADUALLY SPRINKLE IN ALL OF THE SUGAR, 2 TABLESPOONS AT A TIME.

❑ ADD VANILLA.

❑ CONTINUE BEATING (YOU WILL BE LOOKING FOR STIFF, GLOSSY PEAKS TO FORM).

❑ I LIKE TO THINK THAT WHEN MIXTURE HAS THE TEXTURE OF SHAVING CREAM, IT IS DONE.

❑ OVER-BEATING WILL CAUSE THE MERINGUE TO BECOME GRAINY.  KEEP YOUR EYE ON IT.

❑ REMOVE CAKE FROM FREEZER. USING A RUBBER SPATULA, COVER THE CAKE WITH MERINGUE CREATING PEAKS AND SWIRLS.

❑ PLACE CAKE BACK IN THE FREEZER.


YOU'RE ALL SET

❑ PREHEAT OVEN TO 450° AT SERVING TIME.

❑ WHEN APPROPRIATE TEMPERATURE HAS BEEN REACHED, PLACE BAKED ALASKA INTO THE OVEN TO BROWN THE MERINGUE (APPROX. 4 MINUTES).

❑ WATCH CAREFULLY: YOU WANT IT BROWNED BUT NOT BURNED.

❑ REMOVE CAKE FROM OVEN AND PLACE ON A SERVING PLATTER.

❑ TAKE THE HALVED EGG SHELL AND RINSE CLEAN, THEN PUSH DOWN INTO CENTER OF THE MERINGUE.

❑ HALF FILL THE EGG SHELL WITH BRANDY AND DRIZZLE SOME DOWN THE MERINGUE (BE CAREFUL NOT TO USE TOO MUCH).

❑ TURN OUT THE LIGHTS, FIRE UP THE BRANDY AND ENJOY THE APPLAUSE OF YOUR GUESTS.

❑ AFTER BRANDY HAS BURNED, SLICE THE CAKE AND SERVE.

YOU'LL BE A HIT WITH THIS ONE!

# Now, that's Baked Alaska !

INDEX

At Altitudes above 3000 feet, lower air pressure causes differences in the boiling point of water and syrups and also effects baking time.

## Temperature Definitions

180°F(85°C)= Simmering point of water
212°F(100°C)= Boiling point of water
234°-240°F(115°C)= Soft-ball stage for syrups
255°F(119°C)= Hard-crack stage for syrups
320°F(160°C)= Caramel stage for syrups
220°F(108°C)= Jellying point for jams and jellies

## Oven Heats

250°F(120°C)= Very slow
300°F(150°C)= Slow
325°F(165°C)= Moderately slow
350°F(180°C)= Moderate
375°F(190°C)= Moderately hot
400°F(205)°C)= Hot
450°-500°F(230°-260°C)= Very hot

## Roasting Temperatures

Temperatures are most accurately determined by using an instant (microwave) thermometer inserted in the meat.

**Beef,** in the center not touching the bone
130°F(54°C) Rare
160°F(71°C) Medium
180°F(82°C) Well done

**Lamb,** in the center not touching the bone
140°F(60°C) Pink
145°F(63°C) Medium rare
165°F(74°C) Well done

**Pork and Veal,** in the center not touching the bone
160°F(71°C)

**Poultry,** chicken in the breast 170°F(77°)
chicken in the thigh 185°F(85°)
duck in the thigh 180°F(82°)

Egg yolks should always be "tempered" by mixing them with a little hot liquid before incorporating them into a hot sauce. Unless the sauce is bound by flour, don't let it boil again after the egg yolks have been added or they will curdle.

To beat egg whites successfully, always have them at room temperature and use a clean, dry bowl and beaters. A single egg white increases its volume to 1/2 cup, but 3 egg whites will amount to 1 3/4 cups, or 9 times their volume.